VISIBLE
THINKING in the
K–8 MATHEMATICS
CLASSROOM

VISIBLE THINKING in the K–8 MATHEMATICS CLASSROOM

TED H. HULL
DON S. BALKA
RUTH HARBIN MILES

A JOINT PUBLICATION

CORWIN
A SAGE Company

NCTM®

NATIONAL COUNCIL OF
TEACHERS OF MATHEMATICS

CORWIN
A SAGE Company

FOR INFORMATION:

Corwin
A SAGE Company
2455 Teller Road
Thousand Oaks, California 91320
(800) 233-9936
www.corwin.com

SAGE Ltd.
1 Oliver's Yard
55 City Road
London EC1Y 1SP
United Kingdom

SAGE India Pvt. Ltd.
B 1/I 1 Mohan Cooperative
Industrial Area
Mathura Road, New Delhi 110 044
India

SAGE Asia-Pacific Pte. Ltd.
33 Pekin Street #02-01
Far East Square
Singapore 048763

Acquisitions Editor: Carol Chambers Collins
Associate Editor: Megan Bedell
Editorial Assistant: Sarah Bartlett
Production Editor: Veronica Stapleton
Copy Editor: Cynthia Long
Typesetter: C&M Digitals (P) Ltd.
Proofreader: Scott Oney
Indexer: Gloria Tierney
Cover Designer: Karine Hovsepian
Permissions Editor: Adele Hutchinson

Copyright © 2011 by Corwin

Printed in the United States of America

Library of Congress Cataloging-in-Publication Data

Hull, Ted H.
Visible thinking in the K-8 mathematics classroom / Ted H. Hull, Don S. Balka, Ruth Harbin Miles; A Joint Publication with the National Council of Teachers of Mathematics.

p. cm.
Includes bibliographical references and index.

ISBN 978-1-4129-9205-3 (pbk.)

1. Mathematics—Study and teaching (Elementary) I. Balka, Don. II. Miles, Ruth Harbin. III. Title.

QA135.6.H85 2011
372.7—dc22   2010046416

NCTM Stock Number: 14124

This book is printed on acid-free paper.

11 12 13 14 15 10 9 8 7 6 5 4 3 2 1

Contents

Preface

When we educators discuss student learning of mathematics, there is a consistent reference to teaching with meaning, building a conceptual understanding, drawing on previous experiences, and promoting high expectations for success. We say students need these instructional experiences in order to learn mathematics and to be prepared to use mathematics in the workplace. Why do we assume that teachers and leaders do not need these same experiences when they are asked to learn something new and apply the learning in their classrooms? Mathematics teachers and leaders can only initiate change by starting from their current level of understanding and performance.

This idea of moving forward based on one's current level seems to be frequently overlooked. At a minimum, mathematics teachers and leaders experience some form of professional development on an annual basis. Some of the experiences may be directly related to mathematics content and pedagogy, but most of the training is probably more generic in nature. However, the general consensus is that current professional development training is not transferring into classrooms, since teaching in mathematics classrooms remains static (Boaler, 2008).

Continuation of the status quo has strong negative consequences for the future of the United States (National Mathematics Advisory Panel, 2008). To remain competitive in the global economy, our nation needs many more students who are proficient in mathematics. This outcome is unlikely if meaningful change in mathematics teaching and learning does not occur. Meaningful change results when effective, research-based, instructional strategies are used regularly by all classroom mathematics teachers, understood and emphasized by mathematics leaders, and supported by school administrators.

While it is perhaps easy to dismiss some professional development training or activities as not beneficial or useful, there is far too much professional development to categorize every training or activity as such. Something is missing on the sending end, receiving end, or both. There is an absence of "glue" to make the training "stick." This glue, in our opinion, has to do with understanding the ultimate purpose of the training or activities. The theme or rationale for what the professional development learning is intended to do is missing.

Of course, a goal of professional development is to improve the art of teaching with an outcome that more students learn mathematics, thus obtaining equity. While very good and noble, this idea is not specific enough to impact the current instructional strategies being used in classrooms. Furthermore, the focus is on teachers' actions and not on the ensuing students' responses. Teachers may plan and present dynamic lessons, but if students are not participating, only the teachers are involved in the mathematics.

Certainly, teachers' actions are very important but only in light of how students respond to those actions. Efforts at change need to encompass both teachers and students. We believe the key to effective instruction is making thinking visible in mathematics classrooms. For thinking to be visible, both teachers and students must be equally engaged in learning activities. In this book, we show teachers how to achieve this classroom condition and use visible thinking to increase student learning.

OVERVIEW OF THIS BOOK

This book is organized into four parts. In Part I, we establish the foundation for understanding the purpose and rationale for visible thinking. Chapter 1 explains and defines visible thinking and offers supporting research for the concept. Chapter 2 offers the current research on thinking and learning with several themes that thread their way through effective teaching and learning practices. Chapter 3 provides the current reality of mathematics instruction and how some current initiatives may actually hinder thinking.

Part II focuses on how to promote visible thinking in mathematics classes. Chapter 4 explains the relationships among instructional strategies, the resulting actions, and the classroom conditions, all of which directly depend on visible thinking to be effective. Chapter 5 offers very specific suggestions for planning for and achieving long-term instructional improvements in mathematics classrooms. These long-term goals are followed by short-term objectives offered in Chapter 6. The chapter provides a sequential and developmental way for teachers and leaders to effectively initiate and sustain change. Chapter 7 describes our instructional model designed to support long-term goals and short-term objectives.

The three chapters in Part III show how to implement our instructional model at different grade levels. Each chapter offers three problems and supporting lessons based on making thinking visible. Chapter 8 focuses on kindergarten through Grade 2 mathematics, Chapter 9 on Grades 3 through 5, and Chapter 10 on Grades 6 through 8. The book concludes with Part IV, in which Chapter 11 offers advice for ensuring that visible thinking is initiated in mathematics classrooms and that leaders and administrators are working to assist teachers in achieving mathematics success for every student.

INITIATING PROGRESS

Mathematics teachers, leaders, and administrators can no longer leave mathematics learning, achievement, and success to chance. Instructional strategies offered during professional development must first be screened to determine whether they are effective—and then actually implemented. If the strategy warrants spending valuable professional development time to learn, and is designed to help students, then the strategy is worth using in classrooms.

The key to success in student learning in mathematics classrooms lies in making thinking visible. To show how this can be done, throughout the book we have provided numerous examples and scenarios using mathematics problems. The examples not only demonstrate for teachers, leaders, and administrators what visible thinking looks like in mathematics classrooms, but also guide teachers in adapting traditional problems to promote visible thinking. The scenarios present situations in which visible thinking leads to immediate and effective teacher intervention strategies.

Making thinking visible in mathematics classrooms is very doable. We offer a sequential and developmental plan for beginning with current practices—whatever these may be—and gradually, but steadily, initiating successful instructional changes into mathematics classrooms.

Acknowledgments

Corwin gratefully acknowledges the contributions of the following reviewers:

Therese Gessler Rodammer, Math Coach
Dixon Elementary School
Staunton, Virginia

Krystal Glick, K–4 Math Coach
Hanover Public School District
Harrisburg, Pennsylvania

Barbara Kelley, Elementary Math Specialist
Grapevine-Colleyville ISD
Grapevine, Texas

About the Authors

 **Ted H. Hull** completed 32 years of service in public education before retiring and opening Hull Educational Consulting. He served as a mathematics teacher, K–12 mathematics coordinator, middle school principal, director of curriculum and instruction, and a project director for the Charles A. Dana Center at the University of Texas in Austin. While at the University of Texas (2001–2005), he directed the research project "Transforming Schools: Moving From Low-Achieving to High-Performing Learning Communities." As part of the project, Ted worked directly with district leaders, school administrators, and teachers in Arkansas, Oklahoma, Louisiana, and Texas to develop instructional leadership skills and implement effective mathematics instruction. Ted is a regular presenter at local, state, and national meetings. He has written numerous articles for the National Council of Supervisors of Mathematics (NCSM) newsletter including "Understanding the Six Steps of Implementation: Engagement by an Internal or External Facilitator" (2005) and "Leadership Equity: Moving Professional Development Into the Classroom" (2005), as well as "Manager to Instructional Leader" (2007) for the NCSM *Journal of Mathematics Education Leadership*. He has been published in the Texas Mathematics Teacher (2006) *Teacher Input Into Classroom Visits: Customized Classroom Visit Form*. Ted was also a contributing author for publications from the Charles A. Dana Center: *Mathematics Standards in the Classroom: Resources for Grades 6–8* (2002) and *Middle School Mathematics Assessments: Proportional Reasoning* (2004). He is an active member of the Texas Association of Supervisors of Mathematics (TASM) and served on the NCSM Board of Directors as Regional Director for Southern 2. Ted lives with his wife, Susan, in Pflugerville, Texas.

Don S. Balka, a former middle school and high school mathematics teacher, is Professor Emeritus in the Mathematics Department at Saint Mary's College, Notre Dame, Indiana. During his career as an educator, Don has presented more than 2,000 workshops on the use of manipulatives with elementary and secondary students at national and regional conferences of the National Council of Teachers of Mathematics, state mathematics conferences, and inservice trainings for school districts throughout the United States. In addition, he has taught classes in schools throughout the world, including Ireland, Scotland, England, Saudi Arabia, Italy, Greece, Japan, and the Mariana Islands in the South Pacific. Don has written more than 20 books on the use of manipulatives for teaching K–12 mathematics and is a coauthor of the Macmillan K–5 elementary mathematics series *Math Connects*. Don has served as director for the National Council of Teachers of Mathematics, the National Council of Supervisors of Mathematics, and the School Science and Mathematics Association. He lives with his wife, Sharon, in La Paz, Indiana.

Ruth Harbin Miles coaches rural, suburban, and inner-city school mathematics teachers. Her professional experience includes coordinating the K–12 Mathematics Teaching and Learning Program for the Olathe, Kansas Public Schools for more than 25 years; teaching mathematics methods courses at Virginia's Mary Baldwin College and Ottawa University, MidAmerica Nazarene University, St. Mary's University, and Fort Hays State University in Kansas; and serving as president of the Kansas Association of Teachers of Mathematics. She represented eight Midwestern states on the Board of Directors for the National Council of Supervisors of Mathematics (NCSM) and has been a copresenter for NCSM's Leadership Professional Development National Conferences. Ruth is the coauthor of *Walkway to the Future: How to Implement the NCTM Standards* (Jansen Publications, 1996) and is one of the writers for NCSM's *PRIME Leadership Framework* (Solution Tree Publishers, 2008). As co-owner of Happy Mountain Learning, she specializes in developing teachers' content knowledge and strategies for engaging students to achieve high standards in mathematics. Ruth resides with her husband, Samuel, near the Blue Ridge Mountains in Madison, Virginia.

Part I

Preparing the Foundation

1 What Is Visible Thinking?

Visible thinking, the focus of this book, may be described as clarity and transparency in one's cognitive processes. Visible thinking requires overt, conscious, and deliberate acts by both students and teachers. When thinking is visible, participants are aware of their own thoughts and thought processes, as well as those of the individuals with whom they are working. With visible thinking, there is a heightened level of awareness both individually and collectively. There is also a heightened degree of productivity referred to as synergy. Visible thinking occurs routinely in effective business communities during dialogues and discussions, brainstorming sessions, collaborative group situations, and crisis-management scenarios. Effective communication is the basis for effective visible thinking. Ideas are formulated, expanded, and refined through sharing. Acquiring this vital skill should not be left to chance.

True mathematical learning, as identified in numerous reports by the National Council of Teachers of Mathematics (NCTM; 2000) and the National Research Council (NRC; 2000, 2001, 2005), requires visible thinking. Research shows that, in the mathematics classroom, visible thinking is the key to mathematics learning and success. Evidence of visible thinking is apparent during mathematical discussions, explanations, demonstrations, drawing, writing, and other ways that ideas are conveyed.

Students and teachers must think, have awareness of their thinking, organize and clarify their thinking, and then share their thinking. Visible thinking is intentional and manifests itself within classrooms in multiple ways:

- Teachers explain their thinking out loud.
- Students orally articulate their thinking.
- Students listen to other students articulate their thinking.
- Students engage in discussions while forming their understanding.

- Students consciously activate their inner dialogue
  - when reading for understanding and
  - when studying mathematics.
- Students record their thinking by
  - solving problems,
  - keeping journals, and
  - completing projects.
- Students demonstrate their thinking through use of technology, manipulatives, or mathematical tools.

Visible thinking occurs within group settings as well as in individual settings. Experts in a field of study are very aware of their knowledge and are very adept at comparing their knowledge with the needs of a situation or problem. "In research with experts who were asked to verbalize their thinking as they worked, it was revealed that they monitored their own understanding carefully, making note of when additional information was required for understanding, whether new information was consistent with what they already knew, and what analogies could be drawn that would advance their understanding" (NRC, 2004, p. 18). These skills and self-monitoring processes used by experts are the very same ones students need to learn and understand mathematics.

When visible thinking is present in classrooms, students are consciously aware of their current understanding of the mathematical concepts being discussed. They are also aware of these concepts in relation to their previous learning and understanding. When thinking is visible, discrepancies and dissonance are obvious to the students. If classroom conditions support visible thinking through safe, open discussion and discourse, these misunderstandings are also readily apparent to teachers. Immediacy is a very important factor in visible thinking. When the discrepancies are apparent to teachers, the teachers have the information they need to take action—and they can clarify the misunderstandings on the spot.

Yet thinking is all too often invisible in schools, and successful learning depends on reversing this trend (Perkins, 2003). "Fostering thinking requires making thinking visible" (Ritchhart & Perkins, 2008, p. 58). By increasing thinking, motivation to learn is also increased. Visible thinking improves the ability to learn, and the increased ease of mastering a skill, in turn, provides motivation to continue learning.

UNDERSTANDING MATHEMATICAL CONCEPTS

The problem $3 + 4 = \square$ is not a challenge for adults and is certainly not difficult for the educators reading this book. Nonetheless, this problem is a significant challenge for very young children. The problem requires translating symbols (3, 4, +, =, and □) into number concepts (a quantity of three combined with a quantity of four), combining the number sets (seven objects), and translating the newly formed set back into the appropriate numerical symbol (7). Students need to recognize the mathematical symbols, understand the symbolic relationships, perform the requested procedure, and accurately select the appropriate symbol—all abstract concepts.

The concepts within this problem are profound and serve as a foundation for mathematical learning. The process—using symbols to represent and solve problems—is mathematics. However, establishing this foundation solely upon rote recall—when I see the symbol 3, and the symbol 4, with the symbol +, I write down the symbol 7—is like building a house of cards on a ship at sea. All too frequently, a significant wave or swell brings down the house of cards. This wave, referred to in mathematical circles as the "mathematics wall," may be operations with basic facts in third grade, operations with rational numbers in fifth grade, algebraic symbols in eighth grade, or any of the thousands of interrelated mathematical concepts, skills, and procedures. One thing is certainly known. Far too many students hit the mathematics wall at a very young age, most likely around third grade (Boaler, 2008). Obviously, if mathematics achievement is to improve across all cultures and grade levels, this wall cannot remain standing.

THINKING AS A MATHEMATICAL PREMISE

Mathematics educators have come to recognize that the key to removing the mathematics wall is found in the following premise:

Thinking is a requirement for learning mathematics.

The question derived from this premise, *Is thinking a requirement for learning mathematics?* leads to additional questions:

- What is mathematical thinking?
- Who needs to do the thinking?
- Can mathematical thinking be taught?
- Does all of mathematics require thinking?
- Is thinking about mathematics natural or manufactured?
- Is there one correct thinking process, or are there multitudes of processes?

These are but a few of the questions that arise when teachers and leaders reflect on mathematical thinking. One thing is very clear. This premise, when understood and taken to heart by teachers, can improve teaching methods and, subsequently, have a career-changing impact. When thinking is recognized and accepted as an essential component of learning mathematics, classrooms must change. If thinking is not intentionally planned to occur, then thinking most likely does not occur for a majority of the mathematics students. Perhaps additional information about student thinking is needed to reinforce this premise.

In the NCTM (2000) *Principles and Standards*, we read, "Students should have frequent opportunities to formulate, grapple with, and solve complex problems that require a significant amount of effort and should then be encouraged to reflect on their thinking" (p. 52). Furthermore, "mathematical thinking and reasoning skills, including making conjectures and developing sound deductive arguments, are important because they serve as a basis for developing new insights and promoting further study" (p. 15).

Beginning in Grade 2, students are often asked to work problems such as the one provided in Example 1.1. Insight into visible thinking is gained from reviewing and reflecting on typical responses to such a problem and on alternatives to the problem.

Example 1.1   Coin Problem

I have 3 coins, a nickel, a quarter, and a dime. How much money do I have?

A. 15¢   B. 30¢   C. 40¢   D. 45¢

The answer is 40¢, and the discussion is over.

There is nothing wrong with this problem if it is used to assess acquisition of knowledge at the requested level. The problem falls far short if used to introduce and promote original or early learning about money concepts and computation with money. There is no time or inclination to think about the mathematics. The focus is on operational procedures for an answer. To address these issues, Example 1.2 provides an alternative.

Example 1.2   Alternative Coin Problem

I have 5 coins in my pocket. The coins may only be pennies, nickels, dimes, or quarters. I reach into my pocket and pull out 3 coins. How much money might I have in my hand?

- *What are some different ways I could have 5 coins in my pocket?*
- *With 3 coins, what is the smallest amount of money I might have in my hand?*
- *With 3 coins, what is the largest amount of money I might have in my hand?*

Multiple ideas, discussion, justification, thinking, reasoning, and problem interpretation are the important points. There are numerous correct answers, and minimum incorrect ones. For instance, one student may answer that the smallest amount of money is 3¢ (three pennies), while another student may respond with 16¢ (a penny, a nickel, and a dime). Often, simple changes in the wording of the problems presented or the questions asked provide opportunities for making student thinking visible in mathematics classrooms. The alternative problem becomes a rich one, with multiple entry points for students with a variety of mathematical backgrounds. We will explore the use of this problem further in Chapter 2.

There is tremendous support for an answer of yes to the premise question, *Is thinking a requirement for learning mathematics?* The *Common Core State Standards* (2010) identify practices for students' proficiently learning mathematics. These practices include such elements as making sense, perseverance, abstract quantitative reasoning, constructing arguments, critiquing thinking, and looking for and using patterns. Visible thinking enhances these practices.

Furthermore, the NCTM (2000) *Principles and Standards* states, "The first five Standards describe mathematical content goals in the areas of number and operation, algebra, geometry, measurement, and data analysis and probability. The next five Standards address the processes of problem solving, reasoning and proof, connections, communication, and representation" (p. 7). By identifying and clarifying these process standards, NCTM has taken a clear stand on the position of thinking in mathematics.

Clearly, half of the standards are identified as process ones. These processes encourage students to actively engage in thinking while learning the content contained in the other half of the standards. These standards address the processes—communicating, reasoning, making connections, problem solving, and creating representations—that make mathematics interesting, engaging, and exciting for students. As noted by the NCTM (2009, p. 3) in its position statement *Focus on High School Mathematics: Reasoning and Sense Making*, they are all visible forms of the act of making sense of mathematics.

We want to take a closer look at the NCTM process standards in relation to visible thinking. Effective *communication* is important to thinking and learning. Students need to be able to clearly and precisely explain their thoughts to other students and to their teachers. Also important is the students' ability to conduct effective internal dialogues. This metacognitive ability, the process of thinking about thinking, is important. Metacognition is internal and external. Because it is often internal for many teachers, students may not be aware of how important the process is in learning without direct teacher intervention (NRC, 2000). As Van de Walle (2004) explains, "Metacognition refers to conscious monitoring (being aware of how and why you are doing something) and regulation (choosing to do something or deciding to make changes) of your own thought process" (p. 54). Standing back and observing one's own thinking process is an important skill for learners (Loucks-Horsley, Love, Stiles, Mundry, & Hewson, 2003). Being aware of one's thinking promotes *reasoning* and forms more solid *connections* between and among mathematics skills and concepts.

Reasoning and making connections are key in learning mathematics. Many of the ideas that are expressed in the NCTM document about reasoning and sense making go hand in hand with ideas we relate about visible thinking: exploring, conjecturing, explaining, and connecting mathematics to existing knowledge.

Problem solving in mathematics generates many positive attributes for students. Students learn to persist because they have more than one way to analyze and solve problems. They gain confidence through being successful. They are able to transfer knowledge into new and novel situations (NCTM, 2000). Through problem solving, students gain facility in translating mathematical *representations* into real-world situations.

VISIBLE THINKING IN CLASSROOMS

We have absolutely no doubt that thinking is required for learning mathematics. The acquisition of mathematical knowledge is vastly different from the acquisition of language. While students do informally acquire some mathematical concepts, such as ideas of shapes, numbers, and measurement, mathematical knowledge, as a whole, is received through formal instruction. Successful acquisition of mathematical knowledge, usable concepts and skills, requires sustained thinking over time. The NCTM (2009) suggests that students need to develop reasoning habits or ways of thinking that become commonplace in inquiry and sense making.

If this is true, then formal education processes must employ strategies and techniques that make student thinking visible to both students and teachers. In other words, in effective classrooms, students' thinking is made visible and feedback is provided. "Given the goal of learning with understanding, assessments and feedback must focus on understanding and not only memory for procedures or facts" (NRC, 2000, p. 128). Failure of instructors to understand student thinking, connections, and conceptual understandings results in learning disasters. An example appropriate for Grade 7 is provided in Example 1.3.

Example 1.3 Proportion Problem

Jill walks 1 mile in 12 minutes, and Jane walks 1 mile in 10 minutes. Jill lives 1 mile from school, and Jane lives 1.5 miles from school. If the girls start home from school at the same time, then who arrives home first?

A. Jill   B. Jane   C. Tie   D. Not enough information provided

---

The problem is intended to be solved by setting up proportions. Jill lives 1 mile from school and walks 1 mile in 12 minutes, so Jill arrives home in 12 minutes. How fast does Jane arrive home? The proportion is

1 mile is to 10 minutes as 1.5 miles is to x minutes

1 mile/10 minutes = 1.5 miles/x minutes

Students solve by cross multiplying and, if they do it correctly, obtain $x = (10 \times 1.5) = 15$ minutes. Jane arrives home in 15 minutes, and Jill arrives home in 12 minutes. So the answer to the problem is Jill.

What if students realized that Jane walks half a mile every 5 minutes, and therefore walks one and one-half miles in 15 minutes? They have correctly solved the problem but are most likely not aware of the mathematics involved in proportions. In order to better understand proportions, students need more time to think and reason. Therefore, they need to remain engaged in the problem.

Students working in pairs on a problem such as Example 1.4 have multiple opportunities to think about and discuss proportional relationships.

Example 1.4 Alternative Proportion Problem

Jill walks 1 mile in 12 minutes, and Jane walks 1 mile in 10 minutes. Both girls live at least 1 mile from school but less than 5 miles from school.

- *If Jill arrives home first, what distance might the two houses be from school?*
- *If Jane arrives home first, what distance might the two houses be from school?*
- *If Jane and Jill arrive at their homes at the same time, what is the closest the two houses can be from school?*
- *If Jane and Jill arrive at their homes at the same time, what is the farthest the two houses can be from school?*

VISIBLE THINKING SCENARIO 1: AREA AND PERIMETER

Continuing through the chapters in this book, you will see that we have provided a variety of visible thinking scenarios for different grade levels at the end of the chapters. The intent of these student-teacher dialogues is to show how visible thinking might manifest itself in mathematics classrooms. A manifestation highlighted in these scenarios is how teachers can use visible thinking to effectively, quickly, and appropriately intervene with student mathematical misunderstandings.

This scenario involves perimeter and area. In many states, students initially encounter the idea of perimeter in Grades 3 or 4 and continue with various extensions into the middle school. Area concepts typically begin in Grades 4 or 5 and also extend into the middle school. In the NCTM *Curriculum Focal Points* (2006), the study of perimeter as a measurable attribute is suggested as a Measurement Connection to the Grade 3 Focal Points, whereas area is listed as a Focal Point for Content Emphasis in Grade 4. Within the *Common Core State Standards* (2010), perimeter is introduced in Grade 3. The concept of perimeter is combined with area in Grade 4.

Even with these early encounters with both ideas, students still lack an understanding of the difference between perimeter and area.

Problem

A rectangle has a perimeter of 64 inches. What are possible areas for this rectangle?

Mathematics Within the Problem

The teacher is helping students understand area, perimeter, and their relationship. She assigns student pairs to work on the preceding problem. The teacher expects students to find areas randomly at first but then become more organized in their approach. As the students organize their thinking, the teacher will investigate and discuss some patterns with her class. She expects students to recall and understand that the perimeter of a rectangle with length l and width w is $P = 2l + 2w$. In the case where the perimeter is 64 inches, students would establish that $2l + 2w = 64$ inches. This is the same as $2(l + w) = 64$, or $l + w = 32$. If only whole number lengths and widths are considered, then students can set up a table such as Figure 1.1.

Figure 1.1 Area of a Rectangle With Perimeter of 64 Inches

Length (l)	Width (w)	Perimeter (P)	Area (A)
31	1	64	31 in.²
30	2	64	60 in.²
29	3	64	87 in.²
.	.	.	.
.	.	.	.
.	.	.	.
16	16	64	256 in.²
15	17	64	255 in.²
.	.	.	.
.	.	.	.
.	.	.	.
2	30	64	60 in.²
1	31	64	31 in.²

The teacher wants students to understand a significant fact relating perimeter and area for rectangles: For a fixed perimeter, the rectangle with the greatest area is a square. For our particular problem, the greatest area is 16 × 16 = 256 sq. in. The teacher is moving about the room listening to students talk and observing their work.

What Are Students Doing Incorrectly?

The teacher notices a student pair has drawn a rectangle and written an explanation, as shown in Figure 1.2.

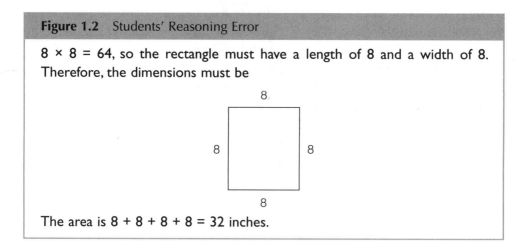

Figure 1.2 Students' Reasoning Error

8 × 8 = 64, so the rectangle must have a length of 8 and a width of 8. Therefore, the dimensions must be

The area is 8 + 8 + 8 + 8 = 32 inches.

What Are Students Thinking and Saying Incorrectly?

The teacher asks the students to explain their thinking in solving the problem. The students share their ideas.

We know that $8 \times 8 = 64$, so this must be the basis for solving the problem. Since the length is 8 and the width is 8, then the area must be $8 + 8 + 8 + 8 = 32$ inches.

The students are distracted by information they know to be true. They know that $8 \times 8 = 64$. Since the perimeter is 64 inches, students have allowed negative transfer to occur. Because they know this fact, they assume it must play an important role in solving the problem. The students are so convinced of this that they let it overshadow other information they also know.

Teacher Intervention

The teacher bends down to eye level and asks the students to look at her. "Without looking or thinking about this problem, I want you (first student) to explain perimeter and you (second student) to explain area."

The first student responds, "Perimeter is the distance around the outside." The second student responds, "Area is the space inside."

The teacher asks the students to turn their paper over and draw pictures that would show the perimeter of a rectangle and the area of a rectangle. The students draw two rectangles and demonstrate perimeter is the distance around and area is the space inside. The teacher asks, "What measurement units are used for perimeter and what are used for area?" Students correctly identify inches and square inches.

The teacher responds with another question that brings visible thinking to the forefront. "If I make the width of your drawing 2 inches, and the length of your drawing 6 inches, what is the perimeter?"

The first student draws a rectangle, labels the dimensions, and answers, "2 plus 6 is 8, plus 2 is 10, plus 6 is 16. The perimeter is 16 inches."

"What about the area?" asks the teacher. Pointing to the rectangle just drawn, the second student gives an answer: "2 times 6 is 12, so the area is 12 square inches." At this point, the first student sees their error and exclaims, "Oh no, I see what we did! For perimeter, we need to find 2 of the width and 2 of the length that add up to 64 inches. So on this rectangle, if the width is 1, then we have a 1 here and a 1 here (indicating the two widths). So that is $64 - 2$, or 62. Half of 62 is 31, so we have 31 here and 31 here (indicating the length). Our perimeter is always 64 inches, and in this case our area is $1 \times 31 = 31$ square inches for the area."

The teacher asks the second student, "Do you understand, too?" The student replies, "I think so." The teacher encourages the pair to work out a few more examples. "Raise your hand for me to check back with you. Both of you need to understand the problem and the solution. I think you have it. That was good thinking!"

> **How did the teacher use visible thinking to intervene and correct a misunderstanding?**
>
> *Students were engaged in a discussion not only between themselves but also with the teacher. They articulated their thinking to the teacher and, as they did so, the teacher was able to diagnose the error in thinking. With students drawing a rectangle and labeling its dimensions, the teacher was also able to understand their thinking and assist them in clarifying the relationship between perimeter and area. She was able to make students aware of their own thinking.*

SUMMARY

In this chapter, we have responded to the question "What is visible thinking?" with the answer "a conscious, deliberate set of actions that provides clear evidence of the current level of student knowledge and understanding." The examples that have been provided shed light on what currently happens in much of our mathematics teaching and how opportunities for mathematical learning can be provided for students when adjustments in our teaching practices are made. Student thinking becomes visible when teaching practices

- Make problem solving and use of problem solving strategies a regular focus of student learning.
- Make students aware of their own thoughts and thought processes.
- Make sharing of mathematical ideas an integral part of lessons.
- Make communication both verbal and written.
- Make student thinking visible in classroom discussions of all kinds.

As we continue in the following pages, many of the ideas that have been suggested in this chapter will be expanded. The purposes and positive effects of visible thinking are identified and explained, as are research-based teacher practices that make student thinking visible. Figure 1.3 offers an overview of the benefits for students of visible thinking.

Figure 1.3 Visible Thinking: Purposes and Effects for Students

Visible thinking increases equity, the opportunity for every student to learn mathematics, by

- Increasing student interest, engagement, and motivation
- Promoting connections to previous learning
- Providing opportunities to think deeply
- Encouraging reasoning and sense making
- Opening dialogue and discourse within the classroom
- Promoting conceptual learning
- Increasing student feedback through ongoing formative assessment
- Supporting belief in effort over innate ability
- Broadening student understanding about learning mathematics
- Promoting student responsibility for learning
- Fostering a community of learners

2 How Do Students Learn Mathematics?

There is certainly a strong link between operations of the brain and thinking and learning. The way the brain works influences thinking processes, memory storage and retrieval, learning connections, ways of gathering data, preferences, and interests. In this chapter, we explore these links and draw out the underlying themes.

WHAT IS THINKING?

Human beings have a remarkable ability to think, reason, remember, and problem solve. The brain processes millions of pieces of information in brief spurts of time as people navigate their way through life. The data stream is continuous during wakefulness. Often, thinking is only attached to conscious decisions such as what to do for lunch—take something, eat out, or skip eating. It is simple enough on the surface, but in the same interval, the brain is sorting through the pros and cons of each decision. What is available to take, how much time is needed, is this tasty or desired, is this healthy, and what is on the calendar for today?

These decisions are only small fractions of the decisions being made by the brain. The brain is also regulating the body, controlling movements, and sorting through interactions and speech from spouses, televisions, phones, children, and perhaps colleagues. The brain, at another level, may be working to resolve issues at work or organizing the day. All the while, all five senses are gathering data.

Educators sometimes forget that students' brains are engaged in similar activities at multiple levels. Their entire focus is probably not on the content material being presented in the classroom. As a result, the content information may be dismissed.

WHAT DOES BRAIN RESEARCH INDICATE ABOUT THINKING AND LEARNING?

Mathematics teachers and leaders do not need to know volumes of scientific knowledge of the brain and how it functions in order to be effective. They do need to know enough to convince themselves, and continually remind themselves, that the actions they take in classrooms directly impact the students' brains and, therefore, the degree of learning. "Students learn mathematics through the experiences that teachers provide" (National Council of Teachers of Mathematics [NCTM], 2000, p. 16). This is true, but only to the extent to which students actually engage in the experiences and intentionally think about the mathematics.

The National Research Council (NRC; 2000) makes three main points about the brain and learning:

1. Learning changes the physical structure of the brain.

2. These structural changes alter the functional organization of the brain; in other words, learning organizes and reorganizes the brain.

3. Different parts of the brain may be ready to learn at different times. (p. 115)

The important message is that learning changes the brain (Jensen, 2008; Willis, 2008), so teaching must promote and use activities that cause the brain to change—and in the intended way.

Information flows through the brain from one neuron to the next through junctions called synapses (NRC, 2000). These synaptic connections are created in one of two ways. First, synapses are overproduced and then pruned. This process tends to occur in the early brain-development years. Second, synapses are added in the brain. This addition process continues throughout the human lifetime.

This knowledge of the addition of synapses is profound; the brain is continually rewiring and remapping itself (Jensen, 2008). These changes in synapses appear to make the nerve cells more efficient (NRC, 2000). This new understanding replaces an old misconception. According to Willis (2008),

One longtime misconception held that brain growth stops with birth and is followed by a lifetime of brain-cell death. Now we know that, though most of the neurons where information is stored are present at birth, there is a lifelong growth of the support and connecting cells that enrich the communication between neurons (axons, dendrites, synapses, glia) and even some brain regions that continue to form new neurons (neurogenesis) throughout life. . . . Once neural networks are formed, it is the brain's plasticity that allows it to reshape and reorganize these networks, at least partly, in response to increased or decreased use of the pathways. (p. 426)

It is human nature to seek to understand and make sense of our world. This continual "making sense" process is learning and requires thinking. Throughout the ages, learning has been essential for survival. How to procure food, water, and shelter determined how long an individual or group lived. While these elements are still vital for life, the need to learn has broadened and shifted. Learning in today's society is deeper and more complex than survival. There is a natural, human curiosity about why and how things work—why and how they work in a fundamental, concrete way, and why and how they work in an abstract, theoretical way. This need has probably always existed, but in modern society, time is provided to explore our natural curiosity. This natural curiosity and desire to learn should never be lost or discouraged, and certainly not by institutions of learning.

Learning and making sense are highly related to opportunities to think. This relationship influences the way we react to or process new information. There are five general ways:

1. Information does not make sense and is discarded by the brain.

2. Information makes sense, but the conclusion is incorrect.

3. Information does not make sense but is remembered.

4. Information makes sense but does not replace prior understanding.

5. Information makes sense, the correct conclusion is reached, and the information is properly stored for future use.

Options 2, 3, and 4 are very problematic for teachers. Incomplete or isolated information constantly interferes with new learning. While Option 1 may first appear to be a problem for teachers, it is actually a blessing. If disconnected and isolated pieces of information are retained, teachers are facing the difficulty of Option 3.

Obviously, Option 5 is the desired situation. To increase the probability of Option 5 occurring more often in students, teachers need to continually improve their use of effective instructional methods. These methods increase student thinking. Information cannot make sense if time is not provided for students to think about the information, test whether or not it makes sense, and clarify their thought processes.

WHAT IS MATHEMATICAL LEARNING?

One of the principles identified by NCTM (2000) in *Principles and Standards for School Mathematics* is the *learning principle.* This principle indicates that high-quality mathematics programs promote mathematical understanding and build factual knowledge, procedural proficiency, and conceptual understanding. Because learning is such an integral factor, component, and purpose of teaching, it seems vital to define and explain learning as a basis for improving the processes of teaching and learning.

As indicated by NCTM (2000), learning mathematics is more involved than merely knowing some facts or performing some calculations. Learning mathematics means an individual is proficient in mathematics. Proficiency is learning at a usable level. It implies fluency, adaptability, and mastery. The NRC (2001) identifies five strands of mathematical proficiency:

1. Conceptual understanding: comprehension of mathematical concepts, operations, and relations

2. Procedural fluency: skill in carrying out procedures flexibly, accurately, efficiently, and appropriately

3. Strategic competence: ability to formulate, represent, and solve mathematical problems

4. Adaptive reasoning: capacity for logical thought, reflection, explanation, and justification

5. Productive disposition: habitual inclination to see mathematics as sensible, useful, and worthwhile, coupled with a belief in diligence and one's own efficacy (p. 116)

These five proficiencies directly link to thinking. *Conceptual understanding* indicates that learners know the "big" picture ideas in mathematics and how individual parts fit within this picture. *Procedural fluency* is only beneficial when the procedure is applied correctly within the appropriate situation. The ability to add quickly and accurately when one needs to divide is of no benefit. This idea blends directly into *strategic competence,* or the ability to apply mathematical learning to real situations. *Adaptive reasoning* requires logical, organized thinking that one can articulate and justify.

The final proficiency, *productive disposition,* is obtained by engaging in the first four proficiencies. Through these proficiencies, students learn that effort, and thinking, are requirements for meaningful and useful learning. Engaging in establishing these proficiencies is highly promoted when thinking is made visible.

The concept of proficiency expands the ideas of thinking and learning. Knowing with certainty when something is learned is certainly difficult, especially if this something is a mathematical concept that cannot be easily explained, defined, or selected from a list. Learning, in a narrower definition, may not change behavior, but learning with proficiency will (Jensen, 1998).

Learning mathematical concepts and skills is not particularly easy, while recalling a few surface-level mathematical facts stored in short-term memory probably is. Short-term memory is exactly what it says—short-term. To move beyond short-term memory, engage working memory, and then store information into long-term memory requires students to be actively attentive and engaged in lessons prepared and presented by teachers. Effective lessons have certain themes that support thinking and, therefore, learning.

Successful teachers redefine their understanding of learning and promote mathematical proficiency. They understand when Jensen (1998) states:

> Finally, if learning is what we value, then we ought to value the process of learning as much as the result of learning. Our brain is highly effective and adaptive. What ensures our survival is adapting and creating options. A typical classroom narrows our thinking strategies and answer options. Educators who insist on singular approaches and the "right answer" are ignoring what's kept our species around for centuries. (p. 16)

Mathematics educators value learning—true learning, learning that is demonstrated in the form of mathematical proficiency. Visible thinking plays a vital role in achieving that proficiency. Mathematics teachers do not narrow student thinking; they expand it. They do not marginalize mathematical concepts and skills but developmentally link and expand them. Connections within mathematics (algebra, geometry, statistics, data analysis) are strengthened, and prior knowledge is used to connect new concepts (NCTM, 2009). Teachers not only expect their students to learn, but they also establish high expectations for themselves. They strive to learn strategies and approaches that facilitate student learning, and they devote their lives to doing so.

WHAT ARE THINKING AND LEARNING THEMES FROM RESEARCH?

In coming to grips with the idea of learning mathematics with proficiency through thinking, several themes emerge. These three themes should be common threads in every lesson and must be carefully considered while planning:

1. Making connections and providing time

2. Making meaning and using prior understanding

3. Developing and sequencing

These themes are highly connected and interrelated, yet each has several unique characteristics.

Making Connections and Providing Time

To separate learning from thinking is difficult, if not impossible. Likewise, justifying why teachers would want to do so is unimaginable. If students do not have time to think about a topic, idea, or concept, how are they to actually learn it? They need opportunities to connect information they are being given to information they already have stored. This requires time, not only time to process but also time to revisit the topic, idea, or concept in a variety of settings and circumstances. In this allotted time, according to the NRC (1999), "A learner needs to see the relevance of the cognitive processes she or he controls, including processes of comparison, evaluating same/different distinctions, categorizing the new problem in terms of what seems familiar or unfamiliar, and so forth" (p. 27). Teachers can surely help point out some of these features, but students also need time to process independently, with a partner, and with a small group.

Making Meaning and Using Prior Understanding

Even though students may connect new information to previously presented information, there is no assurance that this connection, or the information, makes any sense to the students. Educators are well aware of the following statement (NRC, 1999):

> Formal instruction does not easily dislodge students' prior understanding; only by probing for and identifying students' prior knowledge, including misconceptions and misunderstandings, can teachers use instruction to move their students on to more accurate and more sophisticated levels of understanding. (pp. 24–25)

When planning and presenting lessons, teachers know to consider more than just what has been previously presented to students as a basis for building a new understanding. Teachers draw from their experiences, other teachers, and curriculum materials to consider typical misconceptions students have. Aware of these possible misconceptions and misunderstandings, effective teachers are carefully attuned to "student talk" and other indicators.

Developing and Sequencing

Mathematics is developmental in nature, with concepts and skills constantly expanding and connections continually being made. Yet lessons must be taught in a sequential way. Since time only moves forward, teachers have no choice but to design and deliver lessons sequentially. One selected skill must be taught before another. This dilemma is frequently problematic. It causes teachers and material developers to dissect into separate parts various concepts and skills. The parts are delivered sequentially but need to be put together holistically. If the developmental and conceptual nature of mathematics is not presented, emphasized, and repeated, then students may well see mathematics content as they would a passing train—one car at a time. This one-car-at-a-time approach is often reinforced in the daily lesson materials from textbooks. As Marshall (2006) explains,

> Teaching mathematics with understanding means creating experiences in which . . . interconnections can be made because, without them, there would be a real danger that questions put in isolation would make the learning process rather piecemeal and incoherent. What is more, the low retention of fragmentary knowledge is well attested, which again does not help when we need to use the math we learned yesterday sometime far off in the future. (p. 358)

Effective teachers recognize and work to counteract this dichotomy of developmental and sequential. They continually help students put the parts together. In Chapter 4, we directly address this conflict.

Summing Up Thinking and Learning

Based on the information presented in the preceding paragraphs, we can draw the following conclusions about thinking and learning:

- Thinking is the process of consciously engaging the brain to attend to specific content in an effort to make sense of the content, relate it to content from prior understandings, and store the content into memory.
- Learning is a highly complex phenomenon that scientists, researchers, and educators are just beginning to understand from the physical standpoint of the brain.
- Learning of mathematics is a long-term change in the acquisition and application of mathematical knowledge and skill as exhibited by both understanding and behavior.
- What is being learned is reinforced by the teaching strategies employed by effective teachers, especially the use of visible thinking in mathematics classrooms.

EXAMPLE PROBLEMS REVISITED

In Chapter 1, two problems were provided for study. At that point in the book, the idea of visible thinking was first presented. Since that time, definitions of thinking, visible thinking, and learning have been provided. Now is the time to revisit those two problems to show how visible thinking might begin to take form in mathematics classrooms. Possible solutions and discussions on thinking are provided for each problem.

Example 2.1 Alternative Coin Problem (Example 1.2 Revisited)

I have 5 coins in my pocket. The coins may only be pennies, nickels, dimes, or quarters. I reach into my pocket and pull out 3 coins. How much money might I have in my hand?

- *What are some different ways I could have 5 coins in my pocket?*

In order to work on this problem, students need to have a concept of what coins may be available in the teacher's pocket. Students' inclinations are to arrive at one answer, for example, one penny, one nickel, one dime, and two quarters. They assign the quantity of 1 to each coin type, until they realize they need one additional coin since there are only four types of coins noted in the problem. For young children, the point of this problem is not to find every possible combination but rather for them to understand that multiple combinations exist. For older students, however, the point of the problem may be to find every possible combination. Here are some representative combinations:

> 2 pennies, 1 nickel, 1 dime, 1 quarter
> 1 penny, 2 nickels, 1 dime, 1 quarter
> 1 penny, 1 nickel, 2 dimes, 1 quarter

Students may begin with any combination of coins as long as pennies, nickels, dimes, or quarters are used and they have named five coins. This is an important first step and one that every student can successfully complete.

With 3 coins, what is the smallest amount of money I might have in my hand?

This is a more challenging problem than it initially appears. With the combinations listed above, every denomination is present. The problem does not require this to be the case. For the smallest possible amount in the teacher's pocket, with each coin represented, the answer is 2 pennies, 1 nickel, 1 dime, and 1 quarter, or 42¢. Since the teacher only pulls out three coins, the answer becomes 2 pennies and 1 nickel, or 7¢. Suppose, however, that all four types of coins are not represented. For example, all the coins in the teacher's pocket may be pennies. If this is the case, the answer to this problem is 3¢.

There is no incorrect response to this problem as long as students can justify their thinking and correctly compute the amount of coins. Although the question is simply stated, finding all of the solutions remains challenging. This is not a trick problem but one created to expand students' thinking and reasoning and to compare their thoughts with other students' thoughts.

With 3 coins, what is the largest amount of money I might have in my hand?

By this time in the problem solving process, students may have several additional patterns of thought. The issue for students is whether or not the patterns transfer to a new situation. Some students may persist with the idea that all denominations of coins should be present to the extent possible (answer 1 dime and 2 quarters, or 60¢), while other students capture the idea that all the coins, in this case, could be quarters. The answer then is 75¢.

In the process of working on this problem, students have calculated various sums. They have arranged coins, possibly organized data in tables, and thought carefully about the problem. The teacher can now discuss the problem wording with the students, asking them to explain their rationale for their answer, assuring them they are correct, and then exploring what words clued them to think the way they did. The teachers can ask, "What word or words made you think all coins needed to be represented? What word or words could I change in the problem to make you think differently? If the problem stated . . . , how would that change your thinking?" When the questions are asked, teachers need to be sure wait time is provided, as well as time for students to discuss some of the questions with their partners before being asked to answer.

Example 2.2 Alternative Proportion Problem (Example 1.4 Revisited)

Jill walks 1 mile in 12 minutes, and Jane walks 1 mile in 10 minutes. Both girls live at least 1 mile from school but less than 5 miles from school.

- *If Jill arrives home first, what distance might the two houses be from school?*
- *If Jane arrives home first, what distance might the two houses be from school?*
- *If Jane and Jill arrive at their homes at the same time, what is the closest the two houses can be from school?*
- *If Jane and Jill arrive at their homes at the same time, what is the farthest the two houses can be from school?*

With each question, the problem becomes progressively more challenging. Students can enter the problem at various levels and work to a satisfactory answer based on their skills, abilities, and knowledge. Teachers first want students to visualize the problem. Even though the problem can be worked with computation only, being able to create a representation of a problem is a valuable skill that requires practice. Students should work in pairs or small groups.

Students' first thoughts are most likely linear. In other words, the students will create something like the following:

Figure 2a

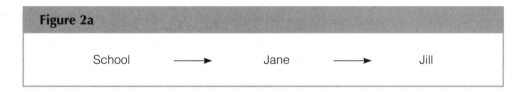

Students probably put Jane's house first because she walks faster. They may have other arrangements. At this point, the representation is not a problem. Teachers then ask students to be sure to place the boundaries of 1 mile and 5 miles. Students create the following:

Figure 2b

School | Jane Jill |

1 mile 5 miles

Teachers may observe some teams of students create concentric circles with the school located at the center. This is sophisticated thinking; students realize the houses may be in any direction from the school. This is not significant for solving this problem and should not be stressed this early in the process. Before assigning the first problem, teachers should expect students to be able to verbalize the situation in their own words.

If Jill arrives home first, what distance might the two houses be from school?

This problem is intentionally not very difficult to solve and does not require significant calculations to find an acceptable answer. Using their drawings, students can place Jill's house on the 1-mile marker. At this location, Jill reaches her home in 12 minutes. Now, the problem is to locate Jane's house. The location must be beyond the 1-mile marker, because the problem states that both houses are at least 1 mile from school. And Jane walks a mile in only 10 minutes; if both houses were 1 mile away, Jane would arrive home first, not Jill.

Students may return to their drawing and locate the 2-mile, 3-mile, and 4-mile markers.

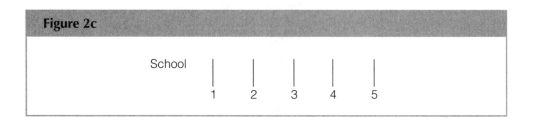

Figure 2c

School | | | | |

1 2 3 4 5

With Jill's house at the 1-mile marker, Jane must walk more than 12 minutes before reaching her home since Jill reaches her home in 12 minutes. Students may notice that Jane may live 2 miles away since it would take Jane 20 minutes (10 minutes per mile) to reach home. Therefore, a possible solution is that Jill lives 1 mile from school and Jane lives 2 miles from school.

If Jane arrives home first, what distance might the two houses be from school?

Once students work through the first problem, they should be able to solve this problem. Since Jane walks faster, both students could live 1 mile from school and meet the conditions. Although this particular scenario seems straightforward, teachers should have students discuss their thinking. Teachers need to be sure students have a clear understanding of the problem situation. Most important, students need to realize that Jill's and Jane's houses can move anywhere within the 1- and 5-mile markers and that solutions do not have to be exactly at one of the mile markers.

> If Jane and Jill arrive at their homes at the same time, what is the closest the two houses can be from school?

Students should conclude that Jill's house should be at the 1-mile marker because that is the nearest place she can live and, therefore, the fastest place she can reach. Since Jill is at her home in 12 minutes, the question becomes, *Where is Jane in 12 minutes?* Students set up a proportion:

1 mile is to 10 minutes as x miles is to 12 minutes, or $1/10 = x/12$

$10x = 12$ or $x = 1.2$ miles.

Students may solve this problem using a chart, as shown in Figure 2.1. Since Jill walks 1 mile in 10 minutes, she walks 0.1 mile every minute. Various solution methods should be encouraged. Students can explain their thinking while comparing and contrasting different solution strategies. In this way, students can determine where Jill is in 12 minutes (10 minutes + 2 minutes, or $1 + 0.2 = 1.2$ miles).

Figure 2.1 Distance and Time for Jill

Jill	
Distance (Miles)	**Time (Minutes)**
1.0	10
0.1	1
0.2	2

Teachers can decide if they want students to convert this result into feet. One mile is 5,280 feet, so 1.2 miles is 6,336 feet ($5,280 \times 1.2$). They need to ensure that students do not confuse tenths of miles and their relationship to feet. For example, two-tenths does not mean 2 feet, 20 feet, or 200 feet.

> If Jane and Jill arrive at their homes at the same time, what is the farthest the two houses can be from school?

Students have now reached the most challenging problem, one that provides a limiting aspect to its solution. In order to solve this problem, students need to think about Jane and her ability to walk 1 mile in 10 minutes. Students may also need calculators to handle some of the tedious calculations. As a result, Jane walks 5 miles in 50 minutes. How far does Jill walk in 50 minutes? Jill walks 1 mile in 12 minutes, so a proportion is set up:

1 mile is to 12 minutes as x miles is to 50 minutes

$1/12 = x/50$

$12x = 50$, $x =$ approximately 4.17 miles.

However, the problem states that both students live less than 5 miles from school. As a result, students must select a distance and time for Jane that is less than 5 miles or 50 minutes. Students may select 49 minutes, or 4.9 miles. Ambitious students may select 49 minutes and 59 seconds, or 4.999 miles (4 miles and 5,274.72 feet).

Where is Jane in 49 minutes? Jane walks 1 mile in 10 minutes, so she walks x miles in 49 minutes: $1/10 = x/49$, or $10x = 49$, so $x = 4.9$ miles (4 miles 4,752 feet).

Jill walks 1 mile in 12 minutes, so in 49 minutes, Jill walks x miles: $1/12 = x/49$, $12x = 49$, so $x = 4.083$ miles (4 miles 438.24 feet).

As noted, the idea of a limit emerges with this particular question. The students live less than 5 miles from school. After some discussion and calculations, students might indicate that Jane could live 4.9999999 miles from school. Students may calculate to the degree to which they are comfortable. Teachers need to allow students to work with reasonable numbers. The important point of calculations with decimals is that students need to understand what the decimals truly mean whether in feet or seconds.

Visible thinking only emerges from this problem if students have opportunities to work with partners or small groups. Assigned as individual work, the problem becomes tedious and overwhelming. As the problem progresses, students should refine their representation of the problem. By moving Jill's house and Jane's house within the drawing, they see the approximations of their calculations.

VISIBLE THINKING SCENARIO 2:
ADDITION OF FRACTIONS

Students first encounter fractions in Grade K and Grade 1, as they study fractional parts of geometric figures. Identifying and understanding fractional concepts is initiated in Grade 3 in the *Common Core State Standards* (2010) and continually expanded through Grade 7. After learning about the relationship between fractions and decimals, students begin work with addition and subtraction of fractions in Grade 5 (NCTM, 2006). Initial understandings relate to addition and subtraction with like denominators. However, students typically have more difficulty adding and subtracting fractions with unlike denominators. They forget about finding common denominators and using the identity element 1 to find equivalent fractions such as $1/3 = 1/3 \times 2/2 = 2/6$ or $1/3 \times 3/3 = 3/9$. One of the most common errors is for students to add numerators and then the denominators such as $1/3 + 2/5 = 3/8$.

Problem

Students have been learning about addition of fractions with unlike denominators for several days. The teacher decides it is time for some practice, as well as an opportunity to check student understanding. She decides to have students play a game involving the concept.

Mathematics Within the Problem

The class is divided into groups of three or four students. A game board and two identical unit-fraction dice are provided to each group of students. Each die has one of the unit fractions ($1/2$, $1/3$, $1/4$, $1/6$, $1/8$, and $1/9$) placed on each of the six faces. With unit fractions, the sum of any pair of fractions from the two dice is not greater than 1 (or $1/2 + 1/2$). The game board is a picture of a step-sided "pyramid." Each step is labeled with possible answers, such as 1, $11/18$, $5/8$, $2/3$, or $7/12$ (see Figure 2.2).

To play the game, a student rolls both dice and adds the unit fractions shown. If the answer is displayed on the next step, the student moves his or her marker to this step. If a student cannot move, he or she loses that turn. Play rotates and continues until the top step is reached.

What Are Students Doing Incorrectly?

Students A, B, and C are in a group and begin playing the game. When it is Student B's turn, he rolls $1/4$ and $1/4$. He correctly determines the

Figure 2.2 Partial Stair-Step Fraction Game Sheet

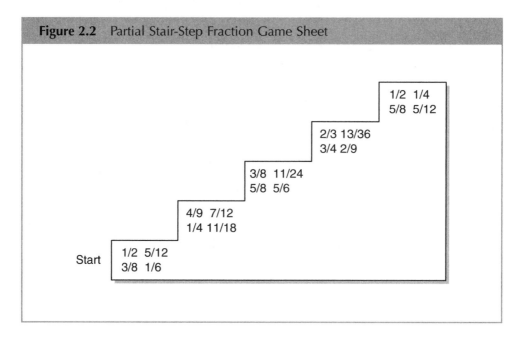

answer is 2/4 = 1/2 and gets to move one step to that answer. When it is Student B's turn again, he rolls 1/4 and 1/8. Student B calculates 1/4 + 1/8 = 2/8 = 1/4 and moves one step up. Student A corrects Student B, by pointing out that 1/4 + 1/8 = 3/8, and so Student B cannot move. Student B says, "My mistake," and play continues.

On his third turn, Student B rolls 1/3 and 1/6. He adds 1/3 + 1/6 = 2/9 and determines he cannot move. Although he is correct in not being able to move, both Students A and C tell Student B that he cannot do that, and Student B asks, "Do what?" Student A explains that both bottom numbers, the denominators, have to be the same before adding fractions. He explains that 1/3 can be renamed as an equivalent fraction by multiplying 1/3 by 2/2 = 2/6. Now, Student B can add 2/6 + 1/6 and get 3/6. Student B says, "Or 1/2. Got it."

What Are Students Thinking and Saying Incorrectly?

On Student B's next turn, he rolls 1/3 and 1/4. He is completely stumped. Student B has two inaccurate strategies he has tried. If one denominator is a multiple of the other, he selects the larger number represented by the denominator (8 instead of 4), but fails to find an equivalent fraction for the remaining fraction (1/4 = 2/8). This is demonstrated in his solution of 1/4 + 1/8 = 2/8. Student B did not convert 1/4 to 2/8; he merely added the numerators and selected the 8. Since the strategy of multiples did not work, he next tries adding across numerators and denominators. This is demonstrated in $1/3 + 1/6 = 2/9$.

Student B, faced with $1/3 + 1/4$, has no strategy left to use since both of his previous ones proved inaccurate. Since 3 or 4 are not multiples of each other, he only has the strategy of adding numerators and denominators. He was fairly sure this strategy would prove to be inaccurate. Nonetheless, he asks Student A and Student C a question:

Is 1/7 the answer to 1/3 + 1/4?

Student C answers no. She explains why and shows Student B how to approach the problem. "First, you need to find a common denominator for the two fractions. I found 12 as a common denominator. Then, you need to find equivalent fractions for $1/3$ and for $1/4$. You can rewrite $1/3$ as the equivalent fraction $4/12$ by multiplying $1/3$ by $4/4$. Then, you rewrite $1/4$ as $3/12$ by multiplying $1/4$ by $3/3$."

Now, Student B adds $4/12 + 3/12$, gets $7/12$, and moves to the second step. Student B has forgotten about common denominators. However, he does know how to correctly add fractions once the common denominator is found (he is not adding $4/12 + 3/12 = 7/24$). Student A and Student C continue to work with Student B during the rest of the game.

Teacher Intervention

As the teacher moves about the room, she hears the conversation in the group. She moves to a group near Students A, B, and C and listens to the explanation Students A and C are providing. Since their information is correct, the teacher allows the game to continue uninterrupted. She makes a note to follow up with Student B. She also walks around the other groups to see whether similar problems in understanding are occurring.

In summarizing the lesson for the day, she emphasizes the need to find common denominators when adding or subtracting fractions. She asks students to get with a partner. She states that she is going to give the students two numbers, such as 3 and 5. She wants the students to write the numbers as denominators of two fractions, $/3$ and $/5 = /$. She then tells the students to find a common denominator. After a brief time, the teacher asks the students to check with their partner. If they agree, flash a thumbs-up, and if they disagree, flash a thumbs-down.

The teacher repeats this exercise with several numbers. After each set, she states the answer. She is watching for any signs of thumbs-down. She notes that Student B is working independently and agreeing with his partner. However, she still intends to have a brief review with Student B the next day during class.

> ### How did the teacher use visible thinking to intervene and correct a misunderstanding?
>
> *By introducing a game format for practicing fraction addition, the teacher provides opportunities for peer tutoring. Other members of the group communicate verbally and in writing how to add fractions with unlike denominators. They are engaged with other students in discussing their understanding of the concepts. The teacher has summarized the ideas involved: Find common denominators for unlike fractions before adding them. To be sure students understand, she provides a quick follow-up to the lessons and the group game.*

SUMMARY

Findings from brain research assist educators in developing appropriate mathematics lessons. In this chapter, we have discussed mathematical thinking and learning and have provided definitions for each term. Both are complex and are linked. Three important themes evolve as we begin to focus on lesson planning where visible thinking is highlighted: making connections and providing time, making meaning and using prior understanding, and developing and sequencing. In revisiting our sample problems from Chapter 1, we begin to shed additional light on how problems might be restated, how questions might be asked, and how students might interact in classrooms where visible thinking activities are common occurrences.

3

What Is Happening to Thinking in Mathematics Classrooms?

Chapter 1 initiated the conversation about the absence of visible thinking in mathematics classrooms, and Chapter 2 identified how students best learn mathematics. Before moving further into the question concerning thinking in mathematics classrooms, several important points need to be made. Educational methodologies and philosophies have gradually evolved over time. The current status of mathematics instruction cannot be attributed to any one particular group, nor has there been deliberate intention to de-emphasize thinking. Current methods of educating students are a result of many cultural, political, and economic factors that have influenced educational practices over many decades. Knowing how educational practices have evolved, while important, is not nearly as important as recognizing where educational practices currently are and need to be. This chapter focuses on where current practices are and identifies some of the greatest influences on instruction.

IMPROVEMENT INITIATIVES AND VISIBLE THINKING

"It is ironic that math—a subject that should be all about inquiring, thinking, and reasoning—is one that students have come to believe requires no thought" (Boaler, 2008, p. 42). In all likelihood, there is a very real disconnect between what teachers believe is occurring in classrooms and what students believe is occurring. Each side has slipped into acceptable roles, adhering to expectations and, usually, following rules and regulations. There are indications from national mathematics studies (National Center for Education Statistics, 2009) that student achievement is increasing in some areas. Improvements have been implemented within schools, and additional changes are promoted and advocated. There are efforts to improve classroom control. States have developed curriculum standards that teachers are required by law to teach. Testing programs such as annual assessments and six- or nine-week benchmarks are instituted by federal or district guidelines.

Each improvement initiative has positive as well as negative sides. In all, they can be used very effectively and derive positive benefits. Ironically, they are also most likely strong contributing factors that impede visible thinking from occurring in mathematics classrooms (Boaler, 2008; Brooks & Brooks, 1999; Jensen, 1998; National Research Council [NRC], 1999, 2004). Yet each of these improvements is very compatible with visible thinking. Revitalizing thinking in mathematics classrooms can be accomplished, but it must be done deliberately. The overall results can enhance each of the interconnected improvements discussed—classroom control, materials and content coverage, testing, expectations, problem solving, and automaticity.

Classroom Control

Classroom management and control serve as a foundation for learning. They also grow more challenging with each passing year. In schools with declining graduation rates, teachers and leaders struggle to keep students in school. They also work tirelessly to provide a safe environment for students. In many cases, these efforts translate into keeping students busy once they are out of the halls and into the classrooms. Cushman (2003) notes, "In such settings, order trumps most other institutional aims. To keep the place running smoothly, students' behavior becomes more important than their understanding, acquiescence more valued than inquiry" (p. ix).

Keeping students busy appears on the surface to decrease interruptions and, therefore, opportunities to disrupt the classroom. Fewer disruptions means a safer and more productive climate. There needs to be a distinction between productive classroom "hums" and disruptive behavior. When does noise generated by students working together reach a disruptive state? What is the balance? To avoid disruptions, teachers may feel that they need to be constantly talking to students or having the students work quietly at their desks (Kennedy, 2005). These actions greatly diminish thinking and erase visible thinking.

Classroom management and control are usually heavily weighted elements in teachers' evaluations. In some situations, school administrators may overtly and tacitly convey to teachers that quiet, orderly rooms are effective classrooms and, therefore, denote effective teaching. They look for and reinforce teaching practices that have teachers actively teaching and students passively quiet or working independently. Observation documents usually focus on teacher actions such as stating the objective, demonstrating problems, explaining problems, moving about the classroom, teaching bell-to-bell, and maintaining an appropriate pace.

Materials and Content Coverage

Covering the required curriculum is truly important. Opportunity to learn greatly increases student success. In every state, students are annually tested over the established standards. Failure to teach some of the content, especially concepts contained on the test, practically ensures student failure. This is a serious dilemma. State documents are generally organized by content strands. In turn, each grade level has concepts and skills arranged for particular strands. These documents are scopes, not sequences.

Even when the scope is rearranged into a sequence, documents provided to teachers promote a checklist mentality or approach. When the National Commission on Mathematics and Science Teaching for the 21st Century (2000) released its report, it revealed a consistency between and among mathematics classrooms. Procedures dominated instruction. Classrooms followed set patterns of reviewing yesterday's work, demonstrating today's work, guided practice, and then independent practice. Teachers asked questions during the lesson, but they were heavily weighted toward low-level knowledge recall. A pattern in questioning was so prevalent that the NRC (2001) named it recitation: "Recitation means that the teacher leads the class of students through the lesson material by asking questions that can be answered with brief responses, often one word" (p. 48). This identified teaching pattern corresponds to the very practices emphasized in observation documents often used by school administrators for teacher evaluations.

The checklist approach to teaching encourages an additional instructional problem. In their haste to remain on target for the established timelines, and prepare students for the next district-assigned test, teachers can easily slip into the operating mode of covering material without real regard for the content. Completing activities becomes the focus of mathematics lessons rather than the mathematical content and concepts supposedly derived from the activities.

Material and content coverage combine to influence classroom management. Teachers feel pressured to cover the prescribed content and maintain classroom control in order to get through the material. Classroom management may take precedence over material and content coverage. When this happens, there is a predictable result. "Student thinking is devalued in most classrooms. When asking students questions, most teachers seek not to enable students to think through intricate issues, but to discover whether students know the 'right' answers" (Brooks & Brooks, 1999, p. 7). The result is the elimination of class time for thinking about, processing, and reflecting on the concepts contained in the material.

The NRC (2002) sums up the situation as follows: "Despite the dramatically increased role of mathematics in our society, mathematics classrooms in the United States today too often resemble their counterparts of a century ago. Many mathematics teachers still spend the bulk of their class time demonstrating procedures and supervising students while they practice those procedures" (p. 3). In other words, many current mathematics teachers teach the same way they were taught.

Testing

The content tested is the content that is deemed important. How the content is tested defines how students believe they need to learn the content and what they need to know. Test formatting also influences teaching. Teachers are admonished not to "teach to the test." Yet multiple-choice tests are fast, easy to grade, and consistent. Everyone is on a timeline and deadline. Textbooks traditionally provide multiple-choice tests for each chapter. District benchmark tests are usually in multiple-choice formats. Technology and data analysis promote and encourage multiple-choice testing. Furthermore, if multiple-choice formats are the tests students must pass at the end of the year, it is unwise not to have students previously experience multiple-choice style tests. As a consequence, tests are routinely given in multiple-choice formats. Multiple-choice tests, as noted above, have a very real purpose. The difficulties arise when multiple-choice tests far outbalance other forms of assessment.

By combining the needs for classroom control, content coverage, and testing, it is easy to see that mathematics instruction has been reduced to a prescription with predictable outcomes. According to Boaler (2008), "Studies have revealed that many math classrooms leave students cold, disinterested, or traumatized. In hundreds of interviews with students who have experienced passive approaches, they have told me that thought is not required, or even allowed, in math class" (p. 42). How can students be allowed time to think within such structured environments? We will respond to this question in later chapters.

Expectations

While much of what has been discussed is newer phenomena in the educational world, the elements are based on history. As mentioned earlier, education has taken decades to arrive at its current position. There are not, however, decades of time available to make adjustments and improvements. Mathematics teachers and leaders need to immediately recognize one very detrimental attitude that strongly influences educational practices. "Historically . . . children have been guaranteed only the right to attend school rather than the right to learn. In fact, the prevalent assumption that has driven public education throughout most of the history of the United States is that few students were capable of high levels of learning" (DuFour, DuFour, Eaker, & Karhanek, 2004, pp. 15–16). The NRC (2002) relates this attitude to mathematics: "Historically, school mathematics policy in the United States was based on the assumption that only a select group of learners should be expected to become proficient in mathematics" (p. 21).

Is this attitude still present? The generally accepted belief is that education has moved beyond this limited view about student potential and mathematics. While this stance is noble, and certainly an important step in change, it does not appear to be supported by reality. The issues raised in the preceding paragraphs indicate that mathematical thinking is not being taught in classrooms. If it is not being actively taught, then why are some students *learning* mathematics and others are not?

First, mathematical thinking is left to chance. Since students in the United States generally work independently, it is left to each student to make sense of the content. Individual learning styles may influence these outcomes.

Second, mathematical thinking is left to situations outside of classrooms. One only needs to look at individual students' support networks to see who is successful. Well-educated parents are able to supply one level of support. Financial status provides another through tutoring, extra assistance, or private schools. Parental expectations are another support, as is time. Students who do not have to work after school, either within the home or outside the home, have opportunities to actually do homework.

The belief about selected students being the only ones capable of truly learning mathematics subtly, and not so subtly, influences educational decisions, such as the establishment of honors and accelerated courses to prepare students for college. The question then is, *Who is left out?* Under the honors and accelerated approaches, a majority of students are. Tracking systems push students toward lower-level courses. Tracking may occur in the elementary grades; however, the practice is fairly widespread by middle school (Grades 6 to 8) and high school. College expectations and aspirations channel students toward course selection. Each of these options sends clear messages to students and teachers about students' abilities to think and reason mathematically. The belief about the selectivity of honors and accelerated courses becomes self-fulfilling for students and teachers.

Most students' mathematics courses become "test prep" courses. Student expectations drop, and now there is evidence that states often lower standards to ensure students pass the exit exams. Urbina (2010) cites John Robert Warren, from the University of Minnesota, who explains, "The exams are just challenging enough to reduce the graduation rate but not challenging enough to have measurable consequences for how much students learn or for how prepared they are for life after high school."

Problem Solving

Problem solving is taught in every mathematics classroom. Textbooks contain problem solving sections with problem solving exercises. State assessments expect students to be able to solve nonroutine mathematics problems. It follows, then, that students are required to think during problem solving lessons. Regrettably, this turns out not to be true.

We have observed that problem solving has often turned into working multiple-choice word problems. There is a huge difference between solving word problems and problem solving. The word-problem approach is procedural. Students are taught word-problem heuristics. These steps are usually something like the following:

1. Read the problem.

2. Circle the numbers.

3. Locate the key words.

4. Determine the operation.

5. Perform the operation.

6. Check the answer.

These steps actually decrease student thinking about problem solving. Often, students skip the first and last steps altogether. They look for visual cues based on their current instruction. If students have been multiplying two-digit numbers by one-digit numbers, then they merely locate the numbers in the problem and multiply. Consider the problem in Example 3.1.

Example 3.1 Procedural Thinking

Mary has invited 12 friends over for a party. She wants to give each of her friends 5 small gifts to open during the party. How many gifts does Mary need to buy?

A. 17   B. 60   C. 50   D. 7

If students are asked to explain their thinking, they actually describe their procedural steps: "To solve this problem, I took 12 and multiplied it by 5—12 times 5. Five times 2 is 10, so I put down the 0 and carried the 1. Five times 1 is 5 plus the 1 that is carried which makes 6. I got 60. Mary needs 60 gifts, so the answer is B." The explanation provides insight into the student's procedural thinking. Yet the explanation does not help with the conceptual thinking. The assumption is that the student multiplied and, therefore, understood the problem.

This assumption may be false. Students rely heavily on visual cues within problems. The preceding problem becomes a challenge once division is included, but only when multiplication and division problems are mixed together. Frequently, when solving word problems, the practice sheet conveniently states something like "practice with division." Students are not reading and conceptually understanding the dynamics of the problem; they are drawing from direction cues and number cues.

Wolfe (2005, p. 177) demonstrates this student approach with the problem in Example 3.2.

Example 3.2 Nonsense Problem A

There are 26 sheep and 10 goats in a ship. How old is the captain?

Students worked diligently on the problem and actually came up with an answer. The experiment becomes more interesting if the problem provides multiple-choice answers, as in Example 3.3.

Example 3.3 Nonsense Problem B

A farmer has 7 cows and 4 horses. How many years old is his son?

A. 6   B. 11   C. 3   D. 7

In the preceding problem, students may use visual cues and key words to select Choice B or 11 (7 + 4, and "how many?"). Students are drawn to multiple-choice answers. If answer choices are provided, students are positive one of the selections is correct. As a result, their reasoning ability is used to find and justify one of the answers rather than to think about the problem.

Perhaps students would draw on their general knowledge or impressions and select 6 or 7 because of their own age. How many students would not answer the question? With mathematics presented in this way, it is little wonder that many students have lost hope and enthusiasm by the time they are in fourth grade (NRC, 1999).

Automaticity

Automaticity is the process of moving skills to an almost unconscious level. Attaining that level of a skill is invaluable. As adults, we do not have time to evaluate, analyze, and calculate 3 + 4 or 3 × 4. Walking, speaking, or driving a car are automatic for most adults, as are many daily routines. Adults can multitask because skills have been automatized. Breakfast can be prepared while holding a conversation or listening to the news or weather. Familiar routines do not need to clutter our brain.

Automaticity is needed in learning. The National Mathematics Advisory Panel (2008) proclaimed that automaticity of basic facts is a major component of future mathematics comprehension. Students do need to be facile with number operations, as well as many equivalent expressions such as $1/2 = 50\%$, $1/2 = 2/4$, $2/5 = 0.4$, and $0.7 = 7/10$. But questions do exist:

- What is automaticity as compared with memory and recall?
- Is there a difference?
- How long or at what age should certain skills reach automaticity, and is it a hard-and-fast rule?
- How much does meaning and understanding influence or regulate automaticity?

These are complex issues that require significant research.

Even though automaticity is desired, it does create problems. This is particularly true for teachers. Once skills have reached automaticity, students appear to have more difficulty in actually explaining their thinking because thinking is really not required. Mathematics teachers are adept at mathematics. They are able to solve a variety of problems without much thought because they have spent years learning to do so. Now, these same teachers must consciously recall their thought processes if they expect to be able to demonstrate for students how to think.

The issues raised above can be observed by revisiting in Example 3.4 Mary and her problem of gift buying.

Example 3.4   Procedural Thinking (Example 3.1 Revisited)

Mary has invited 12 friends over for a party. She wants to give each of her friends 5 small gifts to open during the party. How many gifts does Mary need to buy?

A. 17   B. 60   C. 50   D. 7

How would a teacher explain the thinking used in solving this problem? Even though the problem can be demonstrated in several ways (repeated addition, groups of five, or T-charts), thinking is not really required. The problem selection greatly influences the degree of thinking. What if the problem is restated as in Example 3.5?

Example 3.5   Inviting Student Thinking

Mary is giving a party. She wants to give each invited friend 4 or 5 gifts to open during the party. Mary can invite up to 12 friends. Mary's mother asked her to keep the cost to about $60. What might Mary do?

Students cannot "solve" this problem without thinking, because there is no one solution. They must also carefully read and reread the problem. Automaticity, cue words, and problem heuristics alone do not work in this situation. Students are invited into the problem and are free to state what they would do under different circumstances. Students can perform multiple calculations, rationalize their thoughts, justify their decisions, and explain their thinking.

Teachers need to be aware of automaticity. Mathematical thinking and reasoning need to become overt. Students need to engage and explain their thinking as well as observe teachers engage in problem solving and explain their thinking.

VISIBLE THINKING SCENARIO 3: SUBTRACTION WITH REGROUPING

Mastering multi-digit addition and subtraction with regrouping is a computational skill that is initiated in Grade 2 and continues through Grade 3. The *Common Core State Standards* (2010) initiate multi-digit operations in Grade 2. Understanding the procedures, and eventually the standard algorithm, is increased when students work with mathematics manipulatives or models such as base 10 blocks. These manipulatives help students make sense of the critical addition and subtraction algorithms. For this particular scenario, we focus only on the subtraction algorithm.

Manipulatives are invaluable tools in making thinking visible. Manipulatives are designed to assist students in moving from concrete to abstract understanding. This transfer can only occur successfully when students are highly engaged in thinking and reasoning. By working with teachers, students are able to translate concrete models into abstract understandings. Manipulatives are frequently used in elementary classrooms but not always successfully. Perhaps the relationship between manipulatives and visible thinking has been forgotten.

Problem

The students have been given the problem 324 − 30. Students learned the subtraction algorithm last year but have forgotten how to subtract when regrouping is needed.

Mathematics Within the Problem

Students often have misconceptions when subtracting with regrouping. Some students were taught an algorithm for subtraction with little meaning associated with the skill. The abstract method makes little sense to students who must try to recall rules. The students may memorize rules but use them inappropriately, such as when recalling *always subtract the bigger number from the smaller number* produces the following error:

$$
\begin{array}{r}
324 \\
-\ 30 \\
\hline
314
\end{array}
$$

What Are Students Doing Incorrectly?

The students are not using the regrouping strategy to rename in the 10s and 100s place-value columns. Several students worked out the problem without regrouping and interpreted the answer to be 314. The students need to regroup in the 100s place to rename 324 in expanded notation as 300 + 20 + 4. They also need to understand that 324 can be written as 2 hundreds + 12 tens + 4 ones. Place value and expanded notation are critical ideas. The problem is generally arranged as shown in Figure 3.1.

Figure 3.1	Regrouping for 10s		
324		2 hundreds + 12 tens + 4 ones	
− 30		− 3 tens + 0 ones	
294	or	2 hundreds + 9 tens + 4 ones	

What Are Students Thinking and Saying Incorrectly?

Very few students noticed that sometimes the digits they need to subtract are too large, that is, subtracting 3 tens from 2 tens does not work, as in the problem 324 − 30. They immediately perform a simple subtraction, 3 tens − 2 tens = 1 ten. Some of the students use the term *take away* versus *subtract*, a common practice since that is a phrase they learned in Grade 1.

Teacher Intervention

As the teacher moves about the room, he notices that students lack understanding of the subtraction algorithm. He knows he must make the subtraction example more concrete and less abstract for his students. At this point, he involves all students in a whole-class demonstration and discussion. He invites each student to set up the problem with base 10 blocks.

Each student or partner pair must have a place-value mat in front of them on their desk. This mat will help them recall place value and should look similar to the one shown in Figure 3.2. This place-value mat will allow students to visually label the "unit cubes" that represent 1s, the "longs" that represent 10s, and the "flats" that represent 100s on the board. Students should also write the digit associated with the amount of blocks in each of the spaces.

When the students are ready, the teacher models using regrouping for the problem 324 − 30. Beginning in the 1s column, the students do not need to remove any of the 1s on the place-value board as 4 − 0 = 4. Moving to the 10s column, the teacher should remind students that they cannot subtract 3 tens from 2 tens. Students must regroup from the 100s column, now making the known sum (minuend) 2 hundreds + 12 tens + 4 ones as shown in Figure 3.3.

The students themselves must physically make the trade by renaming 3 hundreds as 2 hundreds and 12 tens. With the 12 tens on the board, 3 tens may be subtracted; thus, the final answer is 294.

Figure 3.2 Forming 324 in Base 10 Blocks

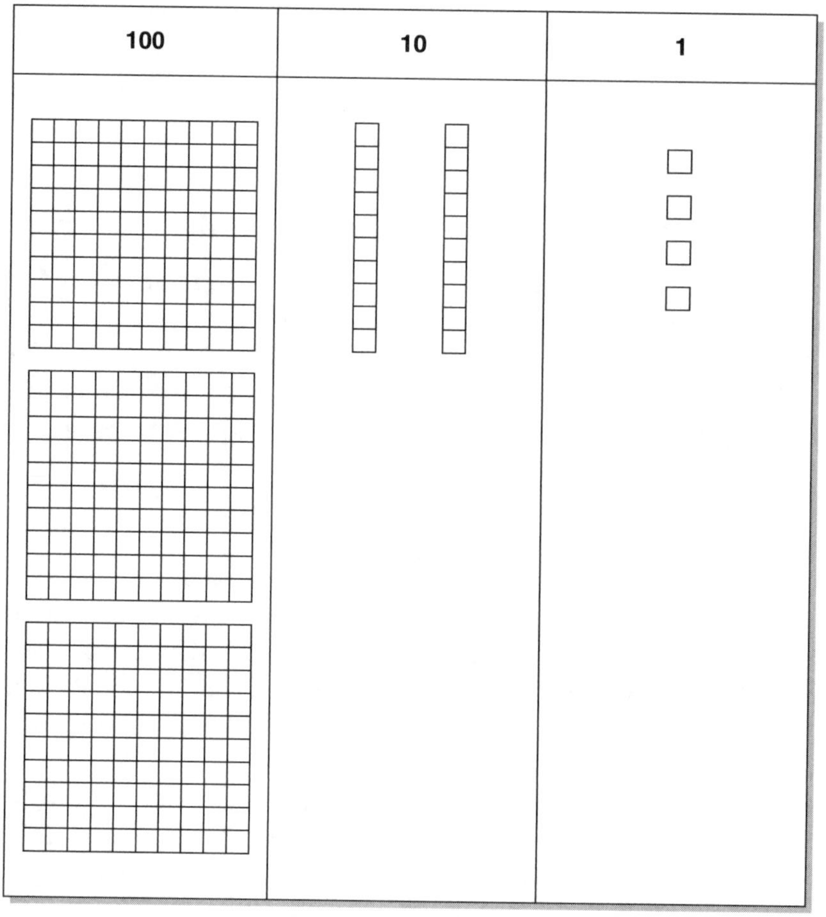

How did the teacher use visible thinking to intervene and correct a misunderstanding?

The teacher used manipulatives to help focus students' thinking. The base 10 blocks provided students a way to express and demonstrate their thinking and afforded the teacher a way to visualize the students' thinking. Students were involved in a demonstration and dialog with the teacher. The teacher modeled the process and was able to help them diagnose their errors in thinking.

A sample dialog between the teacher (T) and student (S) is provided:

T: Look at the 1s column. What do you need to do?

S: Subtract the number 0 from 4.

Figure 3.3 Regrouping 324

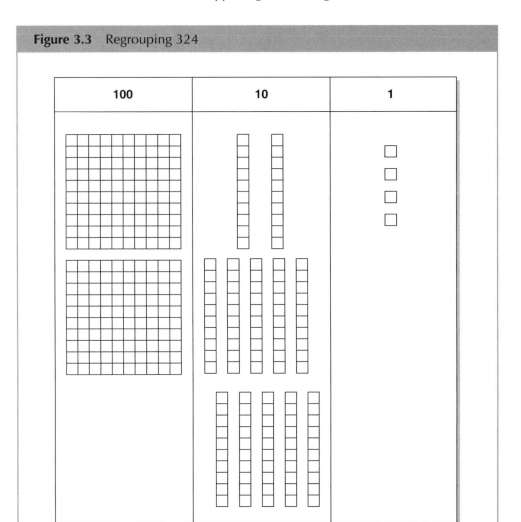

100	10	1

T: Can you show me how you subtract 0 from 4?

S: When I take the number 0 from 4, I still have 4.

T: That's right. When you subtract 0 from 4, you still have 4. Now, look at the 10s column. What do you need to do here?

S: I have to subtract 3 tens from 2 tens.

T: Is there a problem with doing this?

S: I don't have enough 10s.

T: You are right that you do not have enough 10s in the 10s column, but you have lots of 10s. Do you know where?

S: I think the 100s column.

T: How do you have 10s in the 100s column?

S: Well, 100s are made up of 10s.

T: Can you show me what you mean?

S: Ten of these (*pointing to 10s*) is one of these (*pointing to 100s*).

T: That's exactly right. How does this information help you solve the problem?

S: I think I can take 1 of these (*from the 100s column*) and trade it for 10 of these (*10s*).

T: Can you show me?

S: Like this (*student performs the regrouping*).

T: Stop for a second and tell me what you have in the 10s and 100s columns.

S: I have 2 hundreds, and I have (*stopping to count*) 12 tens.

T: Tell me how you got 12 tens.

S: I traded 10 tens for 1 of the hundreds, and I had 2 tens.

T: That is exactly right. Now, do you know what to do next to subtract?

S: Yes, I take away 3 tens.

T: Very good. Can you read the answer to 324 minus 30?

S: Two hundred ninety-four [294].

T: That's super.

Using base 10 blocks, students could see that they could not subtract 3 tens from 2 tens unless they regrouped. By modeling and practicing several problems, the students were able to understand what regrouping means and were able to transfer this skill to the standard pencil-and-paper algorithm.

SUMMARY

This chapter identifies numerous program implementations and initiatives that greatly, and usually negatively, impact thinking in mathematics classrooms. These attempts at improving learning—classroom control, materials and content coverage, testing, expectations, problem solving, and automaticity—are not the sole cause of the absence of thinking. Nonetheless, unless carefully analyzed and implemented, they do exacerbate the situation. By drawing attention to the potential problem, we hope to alert leaders and teachers and demonstrate in the following chapters how thinking can be infused into mathematics classrooms with current practices.

Part II

Promoting Visible Thinking With an Alternative Instructional Model

4

How Do Effective Classrooms Depend on Visible Thinking?

As noted in Chapter 2, the last decade brought about significant scientific brain research, and many of the findings have been used in learning research. Yet there is a vast chasm between research findings and what these findings mean for classroom instruction and who is responsible for implementation.

Many of the factors and findings are highly interrelated, as they should be. There also appear to be some differences among research findings, leading to conflicting reform recommendations. These differences can cause confusion among educators leading a change, as well as those attempting to implement the change. To cut through the confusion, we suggest practitioners think about research-based instruction according to the following three categories: strategies, conditions, and actions. In this chapter, we explain our research-based recommendations for educational improvement and demonstrate how visible thinking promotes the advancement of effective strategies, conditions, and actions, as well as thrives in their presence.

WHAT ARE STRATEGIES, CONDITIONS, AND ACTIONS?

Strategies, conditions, and *actions* are all familiar words to educators, and for our purposes they may be defined as follows:

- Strategy: Careful plan or method of operating
- Condition: Essential environmental requirement for something to operate effectively
- Action: Something that is done or taking place

Strategies are specific skills teachers decide to use in teaching mathematics concepts. These skills can be honed and perfected over time. Actions tend to be broader than strategies and may be the result of numerous strategies. Conditions refer to the classroom climate or atmosphere in which students and teachers operate. Conditions arise from both strategies and actions. Professional development must approach each category as separate but interrelated. For instance, teachers' effective use of questioning (strategy), or continuous assessment (action), is not going to automatically ensure a safe environment. Figure 4.1 provides a list we developed of research-based educational improvements in each category.

Figure 4.1 Categories of Research-Based Instructional Elements

Strategies	Conditions	Actions
Interesting, engaging problems	Safe environment	Opportunity to learn
Questioning	Open discussions	Active engagement
Wait time	Aligned curriculum	Enthusiasm
Manipulatives	Implemented curriculum	Challenging work
Vocabulary development	Metacognition	Class participation
Graphic organizers	Sense making	Technology inclusion
Pair-share	Self-assessment	Connections
Working in groups	Time to learn	Transfer of learning
Peer tutoring	Community of learners	Continuous assessment
Journal writing	Effort over innate ability	Feedback
Rubric scoring	High expectations	Variety of strategies

Why is this organization and information important? How does it help student achievement? The organization serves two important functions. First, it assists mathematics teachers and leaders in understanding that every research recommendation is not a strategy that can be treated as a learned skill, regardless of the amount of training. Second, none of the elements in the three columns are effective without visible thinking occurring. The fundamental purpose for each element is to enhance and encourage thinking.

For the most part, the focus on educational improvements designed to increase student learning and achievement has not been very successful. A strong possibility exists that educators have focused on instructional strategies, and assumed the actions and conditions would naturally follow, or there has been little distinction made between strategies, conditions, and actions when professional development was provided. Classroom conditions such as working as a community of learners are not accomplished by implementing "a" particular strategy but rather by implementing multiple strategies and actions. Classroom environments change when students are provided opportunities to work collaboratively, engage in interesting and challenging activities, discuss their thinking about these activities, and receive positive feedback from teachers.

Another problem also exists. As noted in Chapter 3, thinking, especially visible thinking, is not evidenced in mathematics classrooms. Without emphasizing student thinking, the use of instructional strategies is only superficial and surface level. Surface-level implementation is not going to bring about desired classroom conditions or promote teacher actions based on research findings. We have provided an appendix, Appendix A, in which each strategy, condition, and action is related to the research on which it is based.

There is no one correct way to bring about effective strategies, conditions, and actions in classrooms. Teachers and leaders need to work in ways that feel right to them. However, conditions will probably not develop without strategies and actions being effectively used. For students to feel safe in expressing an idea and explaining their reasoning, they must have opportunities first to do so. When students are encouraged to express their thoughts, and actually do, teachers' responses and reactions greatly influence whether or not students try again.

PRACTICE INTO ACTION

The development of effective classroom conditions has an extremely positive effect on visible thinking, and visible thinking occurring in classrooms has a very positive impact on effective classroom conditions. The following examples illustrate these two points.

Analyzing Multiple-Choice Problems

In Chapter 3, the point was made that current assessment systems and instructional materials focus on multiple-choice items for both assessment and learning. Although a case can be made for using multiple-choice tests as *one* source of data and feedback, this form of assessment does not support original learning, provide time to think, promote connections, engage students, or increase motivation. To stress this point, we analyze four typical problems. The first is presented in Example 4.1.

Example 4.1 Estimation

Bob, his sister, mother, and father take a trip every year to an orchard to pick fresh peaches. They each get their own basket and select their own peaches. When they get back to the stand to pay, they count their peaches. They see that the most number of peaches in any basket is 12 and the least number is 8. What is a reasonable number of peaches the family picked?

A. 20   B. 30   C. 40   D. 50

The mathematical idea assessed is estimating. Since we know that at least 32 (or 8 + 8 + 8 + 8) peaches are in the baskets, Choice A is not reasonable. With the same information, Choice B is not reasonable since it would require some of the family baskets to have less than the minimum of 8 peaches (thus not meeting the criteria of 8 to 12). Finally, Choice D is impossible according to the information in the problem. The maximum number of peaches could only be 48 (or 4 × 12). The intent is to have students understand there are 4 people with about 10 peaches per basket (a benchmark number between 8 and 12). Students mentally calculate 4 times 10 and get 40 peaches. Students then select Choice C.

The second problem, Example 4.2, concerns subtraction.

Example 4.2 Subtraction

Students solve many problems in subtraction. In a subtraction problem there are three elements: known sum (minuend), known addend (subtrahend), and unknown addend (difference). Within a problem, students are confronted with one of the elements being unknown as shown in the examples that follow:

$$7 - 2 = N \qquad\qquad 7 - N = 5 \qquad\qquad N - 2 = 5$$

Each problem type presents certain difficulties to students. A problem with the minuend unknown creates the most difficulty:

Tommy's older brother, Al, collects minicars. Al decided to give Tommy 12 cars. After giving the cars to Tommy, Al had 14 cars left. How many cars did Al have to begin with?

A. 26   B. 2   C. 20   D. 13

In this problem, students set up a number sentence: An unknown quantity minus 12 is equal to 14. This is expressed with a symbol, perhaps a question mark (?), representing the unknown quantity:

$$? - 12 = 14$$

Students need to understand the relationships. Twelve objects (cars) are removed from some unknown quantity, and after doing so, there are 14 objects (cars) remaining. Students need to return the 12 objects to the remaining objects in order to find the original amount of 26 (or 14 + 12), in this case.

The third problem, Example 4.3, focuses on algebraic expressions.

Example 4.3   Algebraic Expressions

Students are asked to work with algebraic expressions. Usually, as evidenced by traditional problems, there is no particular meaning involved in solving the expression. Students merely manipulate numbers and symbols:

Given the expression $3n + 5$, what is the value of the expression when $n = 4$?

A. 12   B. 17   C. 9   D. 11

The expression $3n + 5$ describes a number in a sequence of numbers. If n represents a position of a number in this sequence, which of the following sequences is described?

A. 3, 6, 9, 12   B. 8, 11, 14, 17   C. 5, 10, 15, 20   D. 8, 9, 10, 11

The first problem asks students to perform a substitution and solve. While a necessary skill, thinking is very low level. The second problem is slightly more challenging for students. In this case, students are not provided a value for n. Students need to select a value for n, substitute, and perform a guess-and-check type activity. Students tend to pick 1, but perhaps they selected 2 for n. By substituting, they get $3(2) + 5 = 11$. Answers B and D are possibilities. Students may then select 3. By substituting, they get $3(3) + 5 = 14$. Now, only answer B works. Students should check once more just to be sure. They select 4. By substituting, they get $3(4) + 5 = 17$. This confirms answer B.

Neither of these problems indicates whether students understand or attach meaning to algebraic expressions. For the second problem, the idea of an arithmetic sequence where each term in the sequence is 3 more than the previous term is not apparent. The numerical coefficient 3 in the expression $3n$ lacks meaning for students.

The following problem in Example 4.4, "Sale Price," begins to stretch the thought process even further.

Example 4.4 Sale Price

Students often have difficulty understanding sales-price calculations when presented in mathematical problems. The middle school problem that follows often proves difficult:

> John wants to buy a shirt that is on sale. The original price of the shirt is $30.00. If the shirt is on sale for 15% off, which equation can be used to determine the sale price of the shirt, not including taxes?
>
> A. $s = 30 - 0.15$ B. $s = 30 - (30)(0.15)$* C. $s = 30\ (0.15)$ D. $s = 30 + (30)(0.15)$

Two difficulties emerge for students. First, students have trouble with a 15% discount from an item. Second, students forget to subtract the discount from the original price. In this multistep problem, students usually stop too early. In similar style problems, answers are given rather than equations. For instance, the problem may state:

> John wants to buy a shirt that is on sale. The original price of the shirt is $30.00. If the shirt is on sale for 15% off, what is the price of the shirt, not including taxes?
>
> A. $27.00   B. $25.50*   C. $45.00   D. $4.50

Transforming Problems for Original Learning

The preceding problems are fairly typical and are found in various forms throughout instructional materials. There is an abundance of such problems. While some open-ended questions certainly exist in instructional materials, they do not seem to be sufficient. As a result, teachers and leaders need to understand how to transform or convert these traditional-style problems to be more engaging and thought provoking.

Example 4.5 Estimation (Example 4.1 Transformed)

> Bob, his sister, mother, and father take a trip every year to an orchard to pick fresh peaches. They each get their own basket and select their own peaches. When they get back to the stand to pay, they count their peaches. They see that the most number of peaches in any basket is 12 and the least number is 8. What is a reasonable number of peaches the family picked?
>
> A. 20   B. 30   C. 40*   D. 50

Teachers, or leaders working with teachers, need to open up this problem for students to encourage more thinking. The concept is estimating reasonable answers, not rounding. By having the students select an answer, their thinking can be hidden. Students may first average 8 and 12: $8 + 12 = 20; 20/2 = 10$. They then multiply by 4 and obtain an answer of 40.

Students may also multiply 4 times 8 and get 32. They then multiply 12 times 4 and get 48. Students add 32 and 48 to get 80. Students average by dividing by 2 and get an answer of 40. Both options are correct mathematically but do not assess estimating; instead they assess rounding and averaging.

Students may also get the problem wrong. They may just multiply 4 times 8 and get 32. They do not see 32 as an answer, so they pick Choice B, or 30. They may make the same mistake when multiplying 4 times 12 to get 48. They do not see 48, so they select Choice D, or 50.

Students may also misread the number of family members. As a result, they may select any answer at random. Selecting an answer tends to complete the thinking process for students. Discovering their answer was incorrect does not usually reengage their thinking.

The following revision of the problem is not difficult to accomplish, yet it provides greater insight into student thinking for teachers. Two things are changed. First, the answers are removed. This prevents answers from skewing student thinking. Second, 8 is changed to 9, because finding the mean of 8 and 12, or the answer of 10, is too easy to derive and use in calculations. By using 9, students who perform calculations and round will have rational numbers to work with. Teachers can easily observe this. Here is the transformed problem:

> Bob, his sister, mother, and father take a trip every year to an orchard to pick fresh peaches. They each get their own basket and select their own peaches. When they get back to the stand to pay, they count their peaches. They see that the most peaches in any basket is 12 and the least number is 9. What is a reasonable number of peaches the family picked?

Students should work in pairs. The ability to discuss this problem with a partner increases dialogue and, therefore, thinking. Teachers and leaders need to recall that the focus of these transformed problems is on original learning rather than assessing mastery of prior learning. The answers students derive, and the thought processes used to derive their answers, become very transparent.

Students should identify 4 family members, recognize 10 as a benchmark between 9 and 12, and still reach 40 as a reasonable answer. Without answers available to draw students' attention, they are more inclined to state what they were thinking than how they calculated an answer.

If students multiply 9 times 4 and then 12 times 4, they get 36 plus 48. This gives an answer of 84. At this point, 84 divided by 2 equals 42. If students get 42, teachers have a very clear insight as to how they worked the problem.

Students who decide to multiply 9 times 4 get 36 as an answer. Students who multiply 12 times 4 get 48 as an answer. Teachers need to be aware that students may still round 36 to 40.

Another benefit is derived from open-ended problems. Teachers are given the opportunity to help students understand the difference between rounding and estimating. Rounding is a precise mathematical skill with definite rules and specific answers. Rounded to the nearest 10s place, 31, 32, 33, and 34 are always 30, and 35, 36, 37, 38, and 39 are always 40. Estimating is more concept based. While rounding is sometimes helpful, it is not necessarily the case that rounding derives the best estimated answer. For instance, consider this problem: Each bag of marbles contains 26 marbles; estimate the number of marbles in 4 bags. In this case, students do not want to round 26 to 30, multiply by 4, and get 120 marbles. Students want to multiply 4 by 25 to get an answer of 100. Although 120 is an estimate, it is not a best estimate.

Example 4.6 Subtraction (Example 4.2 Transformed)

Van de Walle (2004), in his book *Elementary and Middle School Mathematics*, identifies three types of problems related to subtraction. There are the result unknown, change unknown, and initial unknown. Students often fail to understand these problem types. The problem illustrated in 4.2 is initial unknown. These prove difficult for students who try to work the problem concretely because they have no total amount from which to begin.

In working subtraction problems concretely, students are familiar with a starting amount (known sum or minuend) from which they remove a requested amount (known addend or subtrahend), and solve for the difference (unknown addend):

John had 10 marbles. He lost 4. How many marbles does John have now?

Students are able to directly model this problem. They count out 10 marbles, remove 4 marbles, and count the remaining marbles for an answer of 6. After working these problems over time, students form some unfortunate habits. They begin looking for numbers, extract the numbers, and perform an operation without reading, much less understanding, the problem.

Teachers need to help students break this habit. Look at the original problem:

Tommy's older brother, Al, collects minicars. Al decided to give Tommy 12 cars. After giving the cars to Tommy, Al had 14 cars left. How many cars did Al have to begin?

A. 26*   B. 2   C. 20   D. 13

Teachers are able to easily transform the problem into one students need to read carefully to answer. The problem can be restated:

Tommy's older brother, Al, collects minicars. Al decided to give Tommy 12 cars. After giving the cars to Tommy, Al had some cars left. How many cars do you think Al had to begin? Draw a picture to describe what you think.

Students are not able to extract two numbers and perform an operation. The only requirement is that Al had more than 12 cars since he had some remaining. Teachers are interested in how students illustrate the problem. How did the students indicate the unknown quantities?

In solving the various types of subtraction problems, teachers want to assist students in understanding the relationships among the known sum, known addend, and difference or unknown addend. These relationships are stressed when students work with fact families:

$3 + 5 = 8$, then $5 + 3 = 8$. Also $8 - 3 = 5$, and therefore $8 - 5 = 3$.

If one of the numbers is unknown ($? - 3 = 5$), the relationships can be used to determine the unknown quantity. Students can be helped to discover, discuss, and understand these relationships by working with problems such as the following:

1. Al had 26 minicars. He gave Tommy 12. How many cars does Al have now? (Result unknown)

$$26 - 12 = ?$$

2. Al had 26 minicars. He gave some to Tommy. Al now has 14 minicars. How many cars did Al give to Tommy? (Change unknown)

$$26 - ? = 14$$

3. Al had some minicars. He gave 12 to Tommy. Now Al has 14 cars. How many cars did Al have to start with? (Initial unknown)

$$? - 12 = 14$$

Problem 3 is directly related to the original problem in Example 4.2. These fact families help students compose and decompose numbers. These relationships do not stop with fact families. The problem concerning Al and Tommy offers the same relationship.

Example 4.7 Algebraic Expressions (Example 4.3 Transformed)

Jeremy wants to go swimming at a local park with some of his friends. He has permission to take his father's van that can hold up to 15 people including the driver. Park fees are $5.00 per vehicle (and include the driver's fee), plus $3.00 per passenger. What will it cost for Jeremy and some of his friends to go swimming at the park?

Students should be provided the opportunity to work with a partner. In this situation, students cannot just substitute into a given expression. They will need to explore the problem by perhaps selecting differing numbers of passengers and deriving a cost. For instance, students may think about Jeremy and two friends. The vehicle is $5.00, and the two passengers are $3.00 times 2 or $6.00. The cost is $11.00. Students may then select Jeremy and three passengers ($5.00 + $3.00 × 3 = $14.00).

Teachers want students to take time exploring the various situations. After students have tried several different situations, teachers should encourage students to find ways to organize the data they are collecting. Perhaps one or more of the student pairs have already organized the data into a table, such as shown in Figure 4.2.

Figure 4.2 Organization of Student Data

Base Fee (Vehicle With One Driver)	Number of Passengers ($3.00 Each)	Total Cost
$5.00	1	$8.00
$5.00	2	$11.00
$5.00	3	$14.00

Once students have been encouraged to talk about the problem and organize their data, they are prepared to begin discussing patterns. What things do the students notice? They may say that the vehicle cost remains constant. They should also note that the total cost increases by $3.00 when the number of passengers is increased by one.

Teachers ask students if they can figure the cost when there are 14 passengers without continuing to complete the chart. Are students able to skip to the problem $5.00 + 14 × $3.00 = $47.00? What would be the cost of this outing if it were a school field trip with a bus full of students? What would be the cost if we did not know the number of students? After allowing time for students to think about the problem, teachers ask students to select a symbol (variable) to represent the number of students. Perhaps students select s to represent the number of students when the exact number is not known. Teachers help students understand the expression: $5.00 + (s × $3.00). Although the variable from the original expression has been changed from n to s, the algebraic expression $3s + 5$ gives the same numerical answers as $3n + 5$. Now, the answer is given in dollars.

Example 4.8 Sale Price (Example 4.4 Transformed)

This problem does not require much change in rewriting. However, teachers need to provide information before the problem is assigned. Students should have the opportunity to observe patterns when taking discounts. Teachers begin by asking students to work with a partner to solve the problem stated earlier, only the discount is 10%. Teachers are looking for student thinking concerning 10% of $30.00 is $3.00. Failure to correctly calculate the discount assures that the remainder of the problem is incorrect. Once the discount is calculated, and teachers are sure students can convert 10% to 0.10, and multiply $30.00 by 0.10, the conversation turns to what is done with the discount.

Teachers next ask students to solve a similar problem, only the discount is 20%. The same procedures as those used previously are followed. Once these two problems are successfully completed, the following problem may be attempted:

> John wants to buy a shirt that is on sale. The original price of the shirt is $30.00. If the shirt is on sale for 15% off, what is the price of the shirt, not including taxes?

At this point, students have a fairly solid idea about sales price and discounts. Students are asked to look back at the problems they have just solved. With a partner, students identify the steps they took to solve each of the problems. They should have the same steps. Several student pairs are asked to discuss their steps. Now, the pairs are presented with the following problem:

John wants to buy a shirt that is on sale. The original price of the shirt is $30.00. If the shirt is on sale for 15% off, what equation can be used to determine the sale price of the shirt, not including taxes?

When students have devised an equation, and several solutions have been discussed, teachers assign the students this problem:

John wants to buy a shirt that is on sale. The original price of the shirt is $30.00. If the shirt is on sale for 15% off, which equation can be used to determine the sale price of the shirt, not including taxes?

A. $s = 30 - 0.15$ B. $s = 30 - (30)(0.15)$* C. $s = 30 (0.15)$ D. $s = 30 + (30)(0.15)$

Teachers assist students in recognizing the various ways the equations may have been written, and then discuss the customary form for an equation. Students should be allowed enough time to assure themselves that their solution steps result in an equation that is equivalent to Choice B.

TECHNOLOGY AS VISIBLE THINKING

As pointed out in Chapter 3, manipulatives, when used effectively, increase visible thinking. By relating what is happening with the manipulatives to what students are saying, thinking, and doing, they are better able to self-analyze and self-check their thinking and understanding. The same outcomes are obtained by using technology, especially calculators, effectively in classrooms.

Calculators allow students to explore patterns without the tedium of performing an inordinate number of calculations. Students may become overwhelmed with procedures and forget to seek generalizations. Two lessons are provided as examples of how technology can enhance mathematics lessons, so students are engaged in challenging problems (see Figures 4.3 and 4.4).

The first sample lesson (Figure 4.3), provided for our use by TI (Texas Instruments & Wilson, 2010), involves visual thinking as a problem solving tool. Whether in the form of a manipulative, a real-world object, sets of objects, a chart, a graph, pictorial drawings, or symbols, these representations are a form of visual thinking for students. But rarely do educators consider visual thinking itself as a formal problem solving strategy or a method for students to communicate their thinking.

Figure 4.3   Using a Graphing Calculator to Model Real-World Situations

2010 Common Core State Standards, Grades 3–8

3.OA9: Identify arithmetic patterns (including patterns in the addition table or multiplication table).

5.G2: Represent real-world and mathematical problems by graphing points in the first quadrant.

6.EE9: Use variables to represent two quantities in a real-world problem.

8.F4: Construct a function to model a linear relationship.

Lesson Objectives

Students use multiple representations of data to model a problem solving situation.

Students will create and use representations to organize, record, and communicate mathematical ideas.

Lesson Activity

"Marie rides her bicycle every weekend at the park. She has trained herself to set a pace of 4 mph. If she maintains this rate of speed over time, what are some possible distances that she could ride each day?" How far could she ride in 7 hours? How far could she ride in 8 1/2 hours?

As noted in the problem above, Marie rides her bicycle at a speed of 4 mph. The illustrations below, taken from a TI-73 Explorer graphing calculator, provide three representations of possible distances for that problem situation. The first screen shows the use of repeated addition, the second screen shows the use of multiplication, while the third screen represents a table of the same data, a result of either of the first two methods.

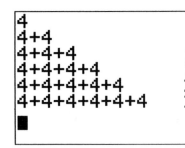
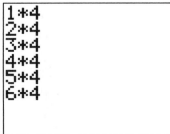

Source: Lesson created by Texas Instruments and Robb Wilson (2010), TI Educational Technology Consultant.

Note: For additional representations with further discussion, please see Appendix B.

Students working in pairs or groups discuss the data and create various models to represent the data. Discussion of the process that students work through is essential to the learning that takes place. Depending on the grade level of instruction, the teacher can modify the level of rigor in almost any problem. For example, in this problem, the speed could be modified to 4.5 mph or 4 1/2 mph to explore various equivalent forms of rational numbers. At a higher grade level, students could be asked to discover how many hours it would take Marie to travel 142 miles, while maintaining an average speed of 4.25 mph, or to graph all of the possible distances that Marie could travel in a 24-hour period.

The second sample lesson (Figure 4.4), provided by Casio (Casio America, Inc., & Pittock, 2010), involves the order of operations and shows how to help students focus on the rules without making calculation errors.

Figure 4.4   Exploring Order of Operations With Calculators

2010 Common Core State Standards, Grades 5–6

5.0A1: Use parentheses, brackets, or braces in numerical expressions, and evaluate expressions with these symbols.

6.EE2c: Perform arithmetic operations, including those involving whole-number exponents, in the conventional order when there are no parentheses to specify a particular order (Order of Operations).

Vocabulary

Order of Operations. Rules that tell how to evaluate an expression. (1) Complete operations within parentheses, (2) do powers or roots (exponents), (3) multiply or divide left to right, (4) add or subtract left to right.

PEMDAS. A way of remembering the order of operations: Parentheses, Exponents, Multiply and Divide, Add and Subtract.

Lesson Objective

Activate students' prior knowledge about order of operations.

Remind students that mathematicians have agreed on this rule to ensure that there is just one answer to a series of computations.

See Appendix B for a handout that may be used for this lesson.

Lesson Activity

If students have not used the acronym ***PEMDAS*** you might introduce it. It is fun to have students make up their own sentences that will help them remember the acronym (***Please Excuse My Dear Aunt Sally*** is a traditional one).

(Continued)

Figure 4.4 (Continued)

Review order of operations using $15 \div 5 + (4 - 3) \times 2^2 = 7$; then have students think, pair, share about other equations until you observe that the students can apply Order of Operations rules correctly.

Give pairs of students equations that are missing parentheses and have them work with each other and a calculator to find how to place the parentheses to make the equations true. (The calculator allows students to focus on the rules without calculation errors intruding on their application.) After all groups have completed at least two equations, offer these questions for a think, pair, share discussion.

- How did you figure out where to place the parentheses?
- When you heard how other pairs figured out where to place the parentheses, did you hear something you would like to do differently? What? Try it and report back.
- Try using order of operations before you put the parentheses into an equation and compare the answer to what the desired result is. Is your answer greater or less? How does that affect how you try to place the parentheses?
- Try another equation using order of operations before the parentheses are placed. Compare your answer to the desired answer, and look for a number in the equation that might affect your thinking about the placement of the parentheses. Describe your thinking.
- Are there any other strategies that you have thought of?

As a final challenge, have pairs write their own equation that uses one set of parentheses, then write it without parentheses and exchange with another pair. Have students describe their thinking about making a challenging equation and how they solved the equation their classmates shared with them.

Source: Lesson created by Casio America, Inc., and Janet Pittock (2010).

VISIBLE THINKING SCENARIO 4: DIVISION

Third grade mathematics has a significant focus on number and operations related to multiplication and division. The *Common Core State Standards* (2010) and the National Council of Teachers of Mathematics (NCTM) *Curriculum Focal Points* (2006) emphasize this focus for third grade. Beyond computational fluency, students need to understand the meaning of multiplication and division. Understandings are increased when students work in problem situations and must make sense of the answers they obtain.

Problem

Students have been working on dividing whole numbers. The teacher decides it is time to determine whether students can use their knowledge of division in a word-problem application. She divides the class into groups of four and proposes the following problem:

> How many cars will we need our parent helpers to drive on our field trip to the museum? We can comfortably seat 4 students in each car. We have 26 children in our class, and of course, I will be going too. I will be riding in one of the cars.

Mathematics Within the Problem

Third grade students often have misconceptions interpreting remainders of a division word problem. Students at this level have learned multiplication facts and can often divide correctly, but they do not know what a remainder really means. If the division of two integers cannot be expressed with an integer quotient, the remainder is the amount left over. The question asked in a third grade word problem can identify the significance of the remainder. This information can often affect the final answer. For example, sometimes the remainder means the answer to the real-world problem must be larger than the quotient.

What Are Students Doing Incorrectly?

The majority of students in the third grade classroom worked out the problem and interpreted the answer to be 6 cars with remainder 3, which is not an acceptable answer to the word problem. The conclusion drawn when interpreting the remainder did not make sense.

What Are Students Thinking and Saying Incorrectly?

One student responded: "We know that there are 27 of us going to the museum, 26 plus our teacher; that means 26 + 1. We have to take our number and put 4 kids in each car. I can show you with pictures, but I can divide it this way." The student did not understand the significance of the remainder shown:

$$\begin{array}{r} 6 \\ 4\overline{)27} \\ \underline{24} \\ 3 \end{array}$$

Teacher Intervention

As the teacher moves about the room, she listens to group conversations of how the problem is being solved. She is looking to see if students can explain, prove, validate, verify, and interpret the results. The following are some of the questions she may ask:

- Why do you think your answer is correct?
- How do you know your reasoning is accurate?
- Can you explain why your answer makes sense?
- Can you verify and prove your answer?

As she is observing the groups of problem solvers, she determines most of the groups have an answer that does not make sense.

At this point, she involves all students in a class discussion and activity. A sample dialog between the teacher (T) and the students (S) follows:

T: Let's pretend we are organizing to go on our field trip. I want you to line up around the wall. Now, how many people are going on the field trip not counting parents? (*Students raise their hands.*)

T: I see everyone's hand is up, and so is mine (*raising her hand*). So how many people is that?

S: Twenty-seven [27].

T: That's correct, 27. How many students can fit into a car?

S: Four [4].

T: We have 27 people going on the field trip, and we can put 4 people into a car, so how many cars do we need?

S: We need 6 because 27 divided by 4 is 6 with a remainder of 3.

T: OK, let's see. I'm going to put you into pretend cars. (*The teacher divides the students into groups of four and then moves to stand with the two remaining students.*)

T: Does anyone see a problem with this?

S: We don't have enough room.

T: Tell me what you mean when you say we don't have enough room.

S: Everyone is going on the field trip, and 6 cars leaves 3 people out.

T: So with this situation, if everyone is going on the field trip, how many cars do we need?

S: We need 7.

In interpreting the results of the answer 6 cars with remainder 3, the teacher asked the children to talk about the conclusion. If a remainder means left over, or left behind, which 3 students will not be allowed to take the field trip? Obviously, the answer to take 6 cars and leave 3 students behind did not make sense. In the dialog among students, they realize another parent would need to drive a seventh car that would include only 3 students. The teacher mentions that all good problem solvers need to go back and reflect on the answer. By doing so, a good third grade problem solver can correct the solution to a division word problem with a remainder and come up with a new solution that makes sense.

How did the teacher use visible thinking to intervene and correct a misunderstanding?

Students were involved in a discussion with the teacher. They articulated their thinking to the teacher, and the teacher was able to help them diagnose their error in thinking. By relating the situation to the classroom, the students were able to understand what "remainder 3" actually meant in this problem: Three students would not be going to the museum.

SUMMARY

Effective classrooms use research-based elements that are strategies, conditions, and actions. These elements foster student visible thinking. Including thinking in mathematics classrooms is not difficult to initiate if it is a true focus and emphasis by teachers. *Deliberate* and *intentional* are key words for making changes in classrooms. These words imply, and mean, that teachers and leaders plan for the change to take place. They also mean that teachers and leaders assess the impact of the planned lessons on students' learning.

5 How Are Long-Term Changes Made?

Positive change in mathematics classrooms can occur over time if leaders and teachers maintain focus on achieving the goal of increasing student success while working to meet short-term objectives. Short-term objectives lead toward the goal when they are aligned to selected teaching approaches, and the selected approaches aid in achieving the goal. The teaching approaches presented in this chapter are drawn from various research findings and are intended to increase student engagement and involvement in mathematics learning. They reinforce effective strategies, conditions, and actions. Objectives, discussed in Chapter 6, are intended to provide markers along the pathway that assist teachers and leaders in successfully maintaining the journey toward their goal and that increase the use of desired teaching approaches, strategies, and actions.

In order to more flexibly fit the needs of different teachers and leaders, this chapter suggests two interrelated ways to consider teaching and learning. One way is to look at the teaching improvement model as presented in Figure 5.1, and the second is to look at the teaching approaches related to the model. Both the model stages and the approaches focus on obtaining effective engagement and involvement of students in thinking. Students need to be aware that learning requires thinking and that thinking is conscious attention.

By focusing on promoting thinking in mathematics classrooms, teachers can use visible thinking as a filter for assessing classroom strategies and actions, which were introduced in Chapter 4. Visible thinking also helps teachers understand a need for specific classroom conditions to exist. These conditions, such as safe environment, learning communities, and open discourse, further thinking. Although they may not be present when initiating a focus on thinking, effective classroom conditions can grow with teacher effort.

ENHANCING STUDENT LEARNING

Teachers need to maintain a focus on the goal of increasing student learning while preparing to teach and teaching. Each lesson is important. Older, established patterns, habits, and behaviors can be difficult to dislodge. These established patterns, even after changes have been made, often reemerge under times of stress and pressure. Hence our emphasis on the goal of student learning while planning, presenting, and assessing mathematics lessons.

Planning, Presenting, Analyzing, and Reflecting

Strategies, conditions, and actions were presented in Chapter 4, and teaching approaches are presented in this chapter. These elements do not just happen, even if teachers want them to happen. They also do not occur at once. Inclusion of these elements in classroom lessons must be intentional and deliberate. Mathematics teachers and leaders have four stages in which to consider how to incorporate the approaches to achieve the goal: planning, presenting, analyzing, and reflecting. These same stages serve as a model to consider for the incorporation of strategies and actions. Figure 5.1 provides an organizational graphic of these stages.

The stages of *planning* and *presenting* are fairly obvious to teachers and leaders. Planned lessons need to focus on how to engage students more fully in the lessons and open up thinking. *Presenting* needs to follow the planned lesson as closely as possible. However, the stages of *analyzing* and *reflecting* may not be as familiar. Analyzing is reviewing the hard evidence derived from instruction:

- What were students able to say and do?
- How did they perform?
- What went as planned?
- What had to be changed?

As much as possible, analyzing should be free of opinion and emotion. Reflecting puts emotions and opinions back into the lesson:

- How did the lesson go?
- How did students react?
- Where were students most engaged and interested?
- Where did they seem to have difficulty?
- Did students learn the desired material?
- What could have been done differently?

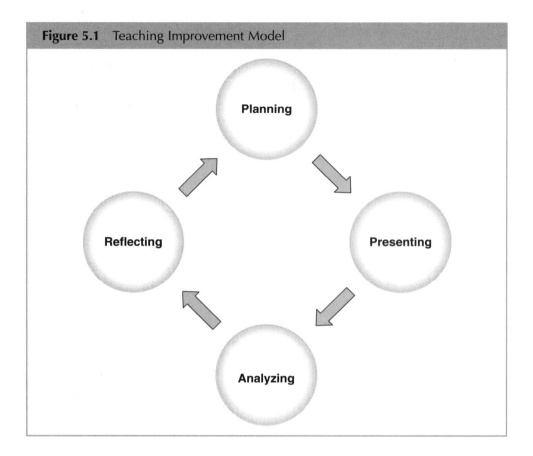

Figure 5.1 Teaching Improvement Model

Reflecting occurs before planning the next lesson and answers two questions:

1. What needs to happen differently when this lesson is taught again?

2. What needs to happen during the next few class sessions to support the learning that occurred?

Improvement efforts may be initiated at any one of the four stages. By looking at Figure 5.1, teachers and leaders should select the stage in which they wish to start and then progress in a circular fashion as indicated in the graphic. For example, teachers or leaders may decide to start at the planning stage. Using visible thinking as a focus, lessons are planned that include problems such as those presented in Chapters 8, 9, and 10. The lesson is presented, analyzed, and then reflected upon. The process may just as easily begin with one of the other stages of presenting, analyzing, or reflecting. If starting with reflection, teachers may think back to when a lesson was taught earlier and may also consider student learning from the previous few days. This information is used to plan, and the process continues.

Understanding Balance in Teaching and Learning

A "universal teaching theorem" that assures all students learn significant, high-quality mathematics does not currently exist, nor does it appear to be on the immediate discovery horizon. This means there is no one prescriptive presentation outline or script for teachers to follow. Nonetheless, we know that there are teaching approaches that increase thinking and learning and those that decrease thinking and learning. Several of these approaches were discovered through teacher trial and error. Additional approaches have emerged through brain research (Willis, 2008). The idea concerning increasing or decreasing approaches toward thinking and learning leads to the notion of balance. Balance, in general, refers to a state where conditions having opposing ideas, qualities, or characteristics are of equal strength or importance.

Mathematics teachers and leaders wishing to improve the teaching-learning process and increase mathematics achievement for all students need to be aware of a balance scale of teaching and learning approaches. On one side are teaching approaches that facilitate and enhance student thinking, leading to increased learning. On the opposite side are approaches that hinder or decrease student thinking, leading to decreased learning. Figure 5.2 provides some examples of teaching approaches to

Figure 5.2 Balance Scale of Approaches to Teaching and Learning

Decrease Thinking ← → Increase Thinking	
Stressing memorization	Promoting understanding and meaning
Emphasizing fact recall	Facilitating usable knowledge
Approaching students as "clean slates"	Addressing preexisting knowledge
Teaching "to"	Teaching "with"
Rewarding quiet behavior	Valuing active engagement
Emphasizing listening	Supporting metacognitive behavior, reflecting
Focusing on procedures	Focusing on problem solving
Telling	Guiding
Providing one example	Assisting in categorization and finding patterns
Focusing on specific detail	Presenting the global network and connections
Requiring independent work	Emphasizing collaboration
Testing for short answers	Supporting thinking and reasoning

demonstrate this idea of balance in the broad goal of enhanced student learning.

The balance scale of approaches is very important. It is not that one side of the scale is right and the other wrong, nor that one side is to be used and the other neglected. A problem arises when one side is being used to the exclusion of the other side—an imbalance. The shift in balance is a consistent, steady shift, not a steep cliff. It is an ebb and flow of various teaching strategies. Understanding student learning requires an understanding of both sides and the balance scale that links them. Many times in American classrooms, the approaches on the increasing-thinking side tend to be underused or perhaps omitted, and the approaches on the decreasing-thinking side are often overused.

This situation requires the scale to be tipped toward increasing-thinking strategies until a balance is achieved. Teachers orchestrate classroom learning activities. "What students learn and how well they understand what they learn depend heavily on the learning activities that teachers devise" (Kennedy, 2005, p. 153).

Examples of such lessons that exemplify strategies on the increasing side can be seen in Figure 5.3 for technology. Provided by ExploreLearning (2010), Figure 5.3 contains a lesson on the square root appropriate for Grades 6 through 8. (Another example using manipulatives can be seen in Figure 5.4.)

Figure 5.3 Using Technology to Find the Square Root as a Side Length of a Square

2010 Common Core State Standards, Grades 6–7

6.EE2c: Perform arithmetic operations, including those involving whole-number exponents.

7.G6: Solve real-world and mathematical problems involving area.

Lesson Objective

A *perfect square* is a number that has a positive integer as a square root. Most numbers are not perfect squares, however, and do not have integer square roots. The ExploreLearning Gizmo allows students to explore square roots.

Lesson Activity

Using the ExploreLearning Gizmo, find the square root of 54.76.

Source: Lesson adapted from ExploreLearning's (2010) *Grade 6–8 Exploration Guide.* Used with permission.

ExploreLearning.com offers interactive online simulations for mathematics and science in Grades 3 through 12. The simulations are called Gizmos. In the Gizmo, there is a shaded square with a tab attached to its lower-right corner. The size of the square can be changed by clicking on and dragging this tab.

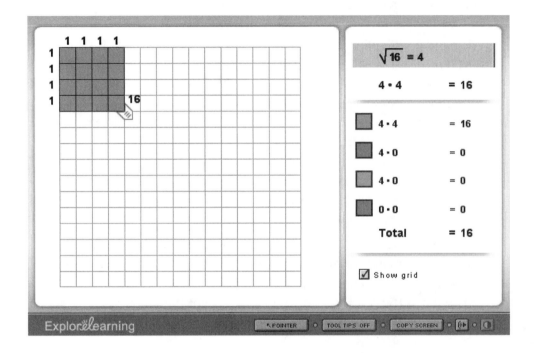

1. Drag the tab until the number displayed beside it is 16. Make sure that Show grid is on.

   a. How many smaller squares are within the shaded region?

   b. Notice the 1 values displayed along the top and left sides of the shaded region. How many 1 values are along the top of this large square? How many are along the left side?

   c. What is the length of any side of the large square?

2. Since the sides of a square are equal to one another, its area can be calculated by finding the length L of any of its sides, and then multiplying $L \cdot L$. The product $L \cdot L$ can also be written as L^2.

   a. What is the area of a square with side length 4?

   b. What is the area of a square with side length 5?

3. Make sure Show grid is on and drag the tab in the Gizmo until the number displayed beside the tab is 6.25.

   a. How many smaller red squares are inside the large square? (Note: although the examples in the book are printed in black and white, the colors we mention here will appear on your screen.)

   b. How many green rectangles are along the bottom of the large square?

   c. How many blue rectangles are along the right side of the large square?

   d. How many smaller purple squares are in the lower-right corner?

4. Make sure that Show grid is turned on and that 6.25 is displayed at the lower-right corner of the square. The area of each of the shaded regions in the square is calculated and shown in the right-hand display. For example, the area of the green shaded region at the bottom of the square is 2 units wide by 0.5 units high, so its area is 1 unit.

   a. What is the area of the red shaded region?

   b. What is the area of the blue shaded region?

   c. What is the area of the purple shaded region?

   d. What is the total area (red + green + blue + purple)?

5. With 6.25 displayed at the lower-right corner of the square, inspect the numbers along the top and left side of the shaded region.

   a. What is the total length of the top of the square?

   b. What is the total length of the left side of the square?

   c. What is the square root of 6.25?

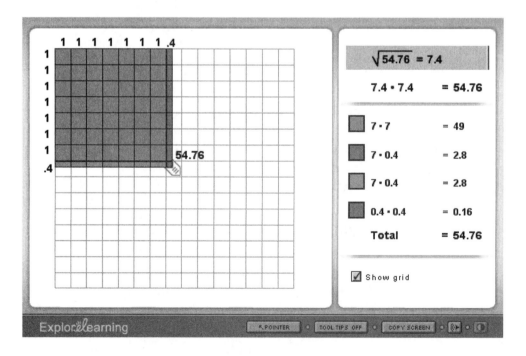

6. Using the Gizmo, find the square root of 54.76.

   a. How does it compare to the square roots of the perfect squares 49 and 64?

   b. Without actually calculating the square root, which two consecutive integers will the square root of 75 fall between? How do you know?

Source: Lesson adapted from ExploreLearning's (2010) *Grade 6–8 Exploration Guide.* Used with permission.

TEACHING APPROACHES

The goal of increasing student learning is supported by teaching approaches identified in Figure 5.2. Teachers and leaders need to recognize the compatibility between achieving the goal and using appropriate approaches. Teachers also need to recognize that the goal and approaches require undergirding strategies and actions (as introduced in Chapter 4 and explained further in Chapter 6). However, these strategies and actions will have minimal positive effect on student thinking and learning if incorporating the approaches is not the purpose.

In emphasizing and clarifying the approaches, several have been selected to highlight. Examples are drawn from the approaches that increase thinking as well as those that decrease thinking.

Approaches That Increase Thinking

In moving classrooms toward strategies and actions, and eventually conditions, that increase student participation and learning with meaning, certain shifts in teaching approaches occur, such as the following:

- Promoting understanding and meaning
- Facilitating usable knowledge
- Addressing preexisting knowledge
- Assisting in categorization and finding patterns
- Teaching "with"

These shifts indicate and imply instructional methods, yet they are broader than selection of specific strategies. They also influence the intent of the lesson, planning, and presenting.

Promoting Understanding and Meaning

Because of schools' systemic structures, it is very easy to start seeing mathematics as a series of discrete, isolated learning objectives. The school day is divided into predetermined time segments, and the instructional materials are designed to work within the structure. Students enter the classroom, the clock starts ticking, the lesson is rolled out, the objectives are reached, the bell rings, and the routine begins anew with the next class of students.

This pattern is repeated five days a week for the entire school semester or year. Lesson flow without disruptions is a critical factor to teachers (Kennedy, 2005). Curriculum content and instruction become like grains of sand in a timer. They run through in a continuous trickle. Yet there are usually grains of sand left in the top part of the timer when the term or school year ends.

This is the reality with which mathematics educators must cope. While perhaps not the most conducive to learning, it is certainly not the least conducive either. Educators debate whether the current system should be replaced by a new one more conducive to how students learn. Mathematics teachers and leaders, however, cannot wait. More important, students cannot wait. Fortunately, there are actions teachers can take within this current systemic structure.

The National Research Council (NRC; 2000) states: "To develop competence in an area of inquiry, students must: (a) have a deep foundation of factual knowledge, (b) understand facts and ideas in the context of a conceptual framework, and (c) organize knowledge in ways that facilitate retrieval and application" (p. 16). These ideas on developing competence are not sequential but concurrent. To be retained, facts must fit within a contextual framework. To be useful, facts must be easily retrieved and correctly applied. A person does not spend significant time learning facts and, then, miraculously wake one day with all the facts neatly organized and categorized. Yet mathematics learning is frequently deemed to occur exactly this way. Periodically, teachers need to help students look at the content "pieces" and put them together.

Facilitating Usable Knowledge

This teaching approach is directly related to understanding and meaning. Individuals who are considered experts have developed an efficient mental retrieval system (NRC, 2002). They have at their fingertips not lists of facts but clusters of related ideas. In mathematics, expertise could be defined as proficiency, implying that mathematical information learned is purposeful and useful. One of the NRC (2000) proficiencies is strategic competence. Usable knowledge does not exist for students who, for example, "know" the multiplication algorithm but continually solve situational problems through repeated addition.

Addressing Preexisting Knowledge

From the earliest age, children come to school with ideas, assumptions, and beliefs about how the world works. "If their initial understanding is not engaged, they may fail to grasp the new concepts and information that are taught, or they may learn them for purposes of a test but revert to their preconceptions outside the classroom" (NRC, 2000, pp. 14–15).

This preexisting knowledge, if accurate, can be engaged to assist with learning and understanding new, related content. Yet this preexisting knowledge, if inaccurate, can directly interfere with learning (NRC, 2005). Students will make sense of the learning within the context of their current understanding.

Students frequently see mathematics as procedural with no logical explanation for how it works (NRC, 2001). As a result, student misconceptions can be, to adults, completely illogical, inane, and nonsensical. Yet to students, they make perfect sense and fit within their understanding. To advance learning, teachers must grasp the current understanding of their students.

Assisting in Categorization and Finding Patterns

Students need time to think, organize their ideas, check their understanding, and verify if their understanding is correct and complete. Metacognition—being aware of one's own thinking processes—helps students monitor their learning (NRC, 2000).

Metacognition and categorization are helped when students create and study patterns and models. Graphic organizers or maps also aid in learning, as do overviews and seeing the "big picture" (Jensen, 1998). In order to categorize, retain, and make sense of the content, students need focused time followed by diffused (additional, spread out) time (Jensen, 1998).

Teaching "With"

Students thrive in classrooms that are communities of learners, where learners and learning are highly valued and respected. In such classrooms, teachers are also learners. They design the learning activities but enjoy thinking with the students. In "teaching with" classrooms, students are challenged to push their thinking: "What do you think happens if . . . ?" Students are free to postulate, guess, surmise, and openly share their thoughts without fear of ridicule. "Teaching with" classrooms have a sense of wonder, an undercurrent of excitement, and enthusiasm for discovering.

Approaches That Decrease Thinking

If the use of certain instructional approaches is going to be increased in order to raise achievement in mathematics, as measured by test scores, then maintaining balance requires that certain other approaches be decreased. To better understand the need for this shift, consider the following statement from the NRC (2005):

> Why are associations with mathematics so negative for so many people? If we look through the lens of *How People Learn*, we see a subject that is rarely taught in a way that makes use of the three principles that are the focus of this volume. Instead of connecting with, building on, and refining the mathematical understandings, intuitions, and resourcefulness that students bring to the classroom (Principle 1), mathematics instruction often overrides students' reasoning processes, replacing them with a set of rules and procedures that disconnects problem solving from meaning making. Instead of organizing the skills and competencies required to do mathematics fluently around a set of core mathematical concepts (Principle 2), those skills and competencies are often themselves the center, and sometimes the whole, of instruction. And precisely because the acquisition of procedural knowledge is often divorced from meaning making, students do not use metacognitive strategies (Principle 3) when they engage in solving mathematics problems. (p. 217)

In making the shift toward balance, approaches such as those in the following list need to be decreased. They increase the likelihood that meaning is lost, and instead of what should happen in Principle 1, 2, or 3, the opposite occurs:

- Stressing memorization
- Emphasizing fact recall
- Approaching students as "clean slates"
- Providing one example
- Teaching "to"

There are arguments that suggest each of these approaches is important. However, when lesson presentations encompass only these approaches to learning, then student thinking and learning suffer.

Stressing Memorization

Memorization is an invaluable skill and a necessary human characteristic. There is information that students need to memorize. Unfortunately, memorization has become the default approach to learning mathematics. It is unreasonable for students to merely memorize every vocabulary word, procedure, algorithm, and theorem.

Memorization consists of short-term and long-term memory. Short-term memory is exactly what its name implies—short term. It is information retained briefly for a specific purpose, and it serves a valuable purpose. It is not essential for people to retain constant streams of information. Although information can be stored in long-term memory, if the information is only memorized, it is very likely not stored with connections. The information, such as a poem or words to a song, can be recalled from memory but not applied or transferred to other situations.

Emphasizing Fact Recall

The issue of fact recall is closely related to that of memorization. This is not a discussion about memorizing basic computation facts. As research from the NRC (2001) clearly indicates, students need meaning and purpose for the information they learn if they are to retain the information. Mathematics learning, while developmental, is not so clearly sequential. In other words, students do not need to have all their multiplication facts memorized and quickly recalled to engage in challenging mathematical problems. In fact, students engaging in challenging problems appear to understand the reasoning behind quick retrieval of basic computation facts and, therefore, better learn the facts. Thus, there is no strong evidence to suggest that teaching of new content must stop until students have mastered basic facts.

Approaching Students as "Clean Slates"

Effective teachers select instructional strategies that fit the content to be taught and the experiences and knowledge of the students. Failure to consider the circumstances under which the learning takes place regards students' minds as neatly erased "clean slates" on which teachers can easily record the designated learning objectives. The students record the information verbatim, store the information intact, regurgitate it on a test, erase their slates, and prepare to repeat the sequence.

Providing One Example

Students need to seek out patterns and organize their thoughts, especially during original learning. This section is not referencing the need for students to practice a skill. Practice is clearly required to acquire mastery. Providing a single example, or type of example, that is unrelated to other knowledge or skills the students might possess reinforces students learning skills in isolation. Single examples with a particular format interfere with the ability to transfer the skill to new or novel situations. Example problems provided in this book allow students to engage in multiple problem situations while maintaining a single learning context.

Teaching "To"

The "clean slate" idea works very well with the teaching "to" approach. Students are assumed to be passive receptors of information, so the job of the teacher is to orderly present the information. In reference to teaching "to," Jensen (1998) states that "teachers who continue to emphasize one-sided lecture methods are violating an important principle of our brain: Essentially we are social beings and our brains grow in a social environment" (p. 93).

We do not mean to indicate that teachers should not provide students with information, nor do we advocate total discovery learning. However, we do refute the idea that students are passive gatherers of disconnected pieces of information to be recalled and used at some later stage in life.

Summing Up Teaching Approaches

Effective teachers seek a balance. There are not instructional approaches that should always be used, just as there are not those that should never be used. When selecting approaches, teachers are to be intentional and purposeful. The approaches should be selected for a clearly defined reason related to student learning. Effective approaches undergird the use of effective strategies and actions and focus on achieving the goal of student learning.

VISIBLE THINKING SCENARIO 5: MIXED NUMERALS

The topic of mixed numerals appears as a Number and Operations Connection to a Grade 6 Focal Point (National Council of Teachers of

Mathematics, 2006) dealing with students' understanding and fluency with multiplication and division of fractions. When students begin multiplying fractions, their misconceptions about adding fractions often reappear, but with multiplication, it works. Yet students still completely fail to understand concepts. In solving the problem $1/2 \times 1/3 = (1 \times 1)/(2 \times 3) = 1/6$, students find the procedure so simple that thinking is not required. Nonetheless, this brief respite from understanding is soon gone when mixed numerals are introduced.

In the following scenario, students are provided an opportunity to explore their understanding of mixed numerals in an engaging problem. The problem encourages teaching approaches such as promoting understanding and meaning, facilitating usable knowledge, assisting in categorization and finding patterns, and emphasizing collaboration.

Confronted with multiplication of mixed numerals, students may just want to find some easy procedure to use. Unfortunately, as in adding fractions, the procedures students sometimes invent are inaccurate. With mixed numerals, students fail to understand the idea about converting a whole number to an improper fraction. For instance, in the problem of $4 \ 1/3 \times 2 \ 1/2$, students fail to rename 4 as $12/3$. They just add 4 to the numerator of 1 and arrive at $5/3$ as an improper fraction for $4 \ 1/3$. Using this same logic, $2 \ 1/2$ becomes $3/2$. Both $5/3$ and $3/2$ are indeed improper fractions, and their denominators fit the problem, so students conclude that their procedure is correct. To complete the problem, students now multiply $5/3 \times 3/2 = 15/6 = 2 \ 1/2$. They do not seem to have made an initial estimation of an answer. Otherwise, they would observe that since $4 \times 2 = 8$, the answer would have to be greater than 8. With this background on students' misconceptions, we present the following problem.

Problem

Kathy and Greg decide to bake a snack. They have a recipe that serves 8, but they only want to serve 2. The recipe calls for 4 1/2 cups of powdered mix, 1 1/2 cups of milk, and 1/2 cup of oil. How much of each ingredient should they use?

Mathematics Within the Problem

The problem requires students to process several pieces of information. The students need to realize that in reducing the serving size from 8 to 2 they are considering only one-fourth of the recipe. The second piece of information is that each ingredient needs to be one-fourth of the original in order for the recipe to have the correct proportions. Students need to work the following calculations:

$4 \ 1/2 \times 1/4 = 9/2 \times 1/4 = 9/8 = 1 \ 1/8$ cups of powdered mix

$1 \ 1/2 \times 1/4 = 3/2 \times 1/4 = 3/8$ cup of milk

$1/2 \times 1/4 = 1/8$ cup of oil

What Are Students Doing Incorrectly?

The teacher assigned the problem to student pairs. Larry and Beth worked together on the problem. They had the following conversation:

Larry: OK, Beth, I think we need to divide everything by 4.

Beth: I agree; do you know how to do 4 1/2 by 4?

Larry: I think so. Let's see. I take 4 1/2; I put the 4 and the 1 together to get 5, and put it all over 2. This gives us 5/2 or 2 1/2 cups of mix.

Beth: That looks right. So with 1 1/2, we add 1 and 1 to get 2, which gives us 2/2 or 1 cup of milk.

Larry: Right. Then we take $1/2 \times 1/4$ and get 1/8 cup of oil. So we have 2 1/2 cups of mix, 1 cup of milk, and 1/8 cup of oil.

What Are Students Thinking and Saying Incorrectly?

The students failed to understand converting a whole number to an equivalent improper fraction. They did not recall or understand that 4 1/2 cups of mix is $4 + 1/2 = 8/2 + 1/2$ or 9/2, not 5/2. They were consistent in their misunderstanding when they converted 1 1/2 cups of milk to $(1 + 1)/2 = 1$ cup. When students worked with the oil, there was no whole number, so they worked the problem correctly.

Teacher Intervention

The students continued their conversation. Since they were working together, and able to discuss the problem out loud, they did have time to think.

Beth: This just doesn't look right.

Larry: What do you mean? I think I did the calculations right.

Beth: Look at 4 1/2 cups of mix. If we just forget the 1/2, then we would need 1 cup of flour for a serving of 2; 4 divided by 4 is 1. And look, when we divided 1/2 cup of oil by 4 we got 1/8. We should have 1 1/8 cups of mix, not 2 1/2. We did something wrong.

Larry: Well, that makes sense, but I don't see what we did.

Beth: I think we didn't get the whole numbers right. Do you agree that 1 1/8 cups of mix is right?

Larry: Let me see, we had 4 cups and 1/2 cup. So 4 cups divided by 4 would give us 1 cup, and we are pretty sure about the 1/2 cup divided by 4 gives us 1/8 cup. Yeah, 1 1/8 cups of mix is right.

Beth: Well, what about the milk? We have 1 1/2 cups of milk divided by 4. Let's take the 1 cup. If we divide 1 cup by 4 we get 1/4 cup, right? We know the 1/2 cup divided by 4 is 1/8, so we should add 1/4 + 1/8.

Larry: Good, 1/4 + 1/8 is 3/8. We need 3/8 cup of milk, not 1 cup like we first figured.

Beth: We know the oil is right, so our answer is 1 1/8 cups of mix, 3/8 cup of milk, and 1/8 cup of oil.

How did the teacher use visible thinking to intervene and correct students' misconceptions?

In this example, the teacher did not intervene in the usual manner. Instead, she provided an opportunity for students to collaborate. Collaboration allowed time for students to think and reason about the problem. Students worked together to self-correct their work and their thinking. They realized that initial estimations for the first two ingredients would give them amounts that are closer to their final answers. This process increased their understanding. By working together, their combined experience and knowledge allowed them to talk through the problem and realize something in their early calculations was not correct. In all likelihood, this would not take place if the students were working in isolation. By working in pairs and with sufficient time to understand the problem presented, students were able to make their thinking visible to themselves. They found their errors in thinking and solved the problem correctly.

As a direct result of this strategy, and an open, safe environment, students were able to self-correct their own thinking and misunderstandings.

VISIBLE THINKING SCENARIO 6: PLACE VALUE

First grade students had been working on writing and counting numbers to 100. The teacher felt the students needed time to reflect on place value and devised a version of Tic-Tac-Toe and Bingo for the students to play.

Problem

Students were formed into pairs and given two 6-sided number cubes, plus two different color highlighters. One of the cubes was blue, representing the 10s digit, and the other cube was yellow, representing the 1s digit. Students were also given a 5 × 5 number grid with 25 numbers randomly selected from the number set 11 to 66.

Students were to take turns rolling the number cubes. Then, a student would align the cubes with the blue on the left and the yellow on the right, read the combined number, and then see if it was located on the grid the pair was given. For example, a 5 rolled on the blue die and a 3 on the yellow die would equal the number 53. If there was a match for 53 on the card, the student would highlight it with a colored marker. The object was to be the first student of the pair to connect the color across the grid, top to bottom or side to side. The color squares did not have to be in a straight line, only touching at a side or a corner (see Figure 5.4).

Figure 5.4 Winner's Number Grid

Mathematics Within the Problem

The teacher wanted to reinforce the idea of place value with the students, involving them in an activity beyond the use of base 10 blocks.

24	15	56	16	26
51	46	25	62	13
43	23	61	31	11
52	22	36	64	55
34	53	21	32	33

What Are Students Doing Incorrectly?

As the students played the game, the teacher walked about the classroom listening to conversations and observing how students were using the dice. Emphasis was on correctly identifying the appropriate number by aligning the dice in the proper order. As he approached one student pair, the teacher noted that the students were quickly covering the squares on the grid. As he observed, he found the students were not assigning the 10s place to the blue die, but reading off the number based on the position of the die. The die on the left, whether blue or yellow, was assigned the 10s place, and the die on the right was assigned the 1s place.

What Are Students Thinking and Saying Incorrectly?

The teacher asked the students to explain the game to him and how they thought it was going. The students readily offered the explanation that they rolled the dice, aligned them (based on position), and read off the number. When the teacher asked them to explain what he meant when the blue die represented the 10s place, the students were confused. The teacher placed two of the same color die on the desk with 3 on the students' left and 5 on the students' right. He asked, "What is the greatest number I can make with these two dice?" One student answered, "35." The other student, after thinking, said, "53." The teacher asked the second student what the 5 in 53 meant, and the student said, "Five 10s." The teacher picked up two dice, one blue and one yellow, rolled them, and asked, "If the blue die is the 10s place and the yellow is the 1s place, what is the number?" The second student answered correctly, but the first student responded, "No, that's not right." The teacher asked the second student if he understood the rules, and he said yes. The teacher asked why he wasn't playing by them, and the student answered, "Because he (pointing at the first student) wasn't playing that way."

Teacher Intervention

The teacher asked the second student to join another group for a few minutes. He asked the remaining student what the 3 meant in the number 35. The student responded, "30." The teacher asked, "What does 30 mean?" The student looked very puzzled and said, "It means 30." The teacher said, "If I said that 30 means three groups of 10, would you understand me?" The student said, "Not really."

The teacher sat down and told the student that they were going to play the game for a few minutes together. The teacher took a sheet of paper and drew a line down the middle of the page. At the top, on the left-hand side, he wrote, "blue, tens," and drew 10 connected squares. On the right side of the paper he wrote, "yellow, ones," and drew 1 square. He asked the student to roll the dice. The student rolled 4 for blue and 3 for yellow.

Before the student could say anything, the teacher asked the student to place the dice on the sheet of paper according to the color.

The teacher pointed to the word *blue* and asked, "Which die goes here?" The student placed the blue die on the left side and the yellow die on the right side. The student said, "43." The teacher stated he was correct and then asked, "How many squares would I draw on this side (pointing left) if I wanted to show 40 (four 10s)?" He counted with the student in groups of 10 stating, "10, 20, 30, 40." The student said, "I would have 40 squares." The teacher asked about 3 in the ones column, and the student answered, "3." The teacher repeated this pattern several times and then called the second student back. He asked the students to continue playing, only to be sure to arrange the dice on the piece of paper before stating the number.

The students continued their play. The teacher moved about the room checking on other students before moving back by the two students to check on their work. They were doing fine.

How did the teacher use visible thinking to correct the misunderstanding?

Because the students were playing a game, the teacher was able to watch and listen. When he detected a problem, he asked a few questions to access the degree of the problem. The teacher quickly determined the second student knew what to do, but the first student was confused. The student was letting previous understanding (position) interfere with recognizing that the blue die represented the 10s place. In his confusion, he had also forgotten what the 10s place actually meant. The teacher wanted to correct these misunderstandings immediately but also reaffirm that position is important. By creating the columns on the piece of paper, the teacher was able to intervene and emphasize critical aspects of place value.

SUMMARY

Teachers are the key element in changing mathematics classrooms (National Commission on Mathematics and Science Teaching for the 21st Century, 2000). But change for the sake of change is pointless. Change without purpose is also pointless. Significant change has two prongs. First, teachers must remain focused on the student-learning goal they are working to achieve, as we have emphasized in this chapter. Second, teachers must begin changing approaches by carefully selecting the strategies to be used in the classroom, as we discuss in Chapter 6. Changes in teachers' strategies result in changes in students' actions and learning.

6 How Are Short-Term Changes Made?

In Chapter 5, we provided mathematics leaders and teachers with broad teaching approaches that promote achieving the goal of increasing students' learning. These approaches add meaning and purpose to mathematics and have a common message of promoting visible thinking in mathematics classrooms. Learning mathematics requires thinking about mathematics. If not in mathematics classrooms, where are students going to learn to think mathematically? Who besides mathematics teachers are better equipped to support students' mathematical understanding and ensure that the students' understandings are accurate and complete?

The long-term goal is elusive and difficult to achieve without some form of map or guide that delineates markers along the pathway. These markers are short-term objectives. Short-term objectives allow teachers and leaders to analyze progress and to make appropriate, timely adjustments. Objectives are selected to support the approaches that increase student thinking.

In this chapter, we guide teachers and leaders in setting short-term objectives by providing answers to such questions as the following:

- What strategies support achieving goals toward increasing student learning?
- Is there an order that works in implementing these strategies?
- What are reasonable and manageable steps in the change process?

PITFALLS AND TRAPS

There is no right or wrong way to move along the path for making changes in mathematics classrooms. Nonetheless, there are pitfalls and traps that can seriously undermine efforts to change. One trap is attempting to change too much at one time. While change does need to be significant in order to make a difference for students' learning, it cannot be overwhelming. Another trap is in making a change without understanding what is supposed to result from the change. What are the expectations from the change, what will students do differently, and what impact will this have on learning? Another common pitfall is not letting students in on the "secret." At the insistence of leaders, teachers may change classroom routines and practices without preparing students. Often, the results are chaos and collapse.

The following recommendation for making changes offers a course of action teachers can take. We have not attempted to explain every possible problem or trap. Further, our suggestion is "a" way, not "the" way. Teachers have various methods, strategies, and activities already in use. They do not need to start over if some of the actions are under way. Also, schools may have their own philosophies they wish to include or stress.

STRATEGY SEQUENCE

The sequence in which strategies toward change (introduced in Chapter 4) may be phased in is shown in Figure 6.1. The assumption behind this suggested sequence is that teachers are not currently using any form of collaborative work with students. If this is not the case, teachers and leaders should make the appropriate adjustments.

Figure 6.1 Instructional Strategies Sequence

Initiating pair-share
Sharing thinking in classrooms
Questioning and wait time
Grouping and engaging problem
Using questions and prompts with groups
Allowing students to struggle
Encouraging reasoning

Teachers need to move at intentional, deliberate speed in implementing these strategies into their classrooms. Depending on the age, maturity level, and previous experience of students, as well as school climate and teacher enthusiasm, the entire transitional process may take from four to six weeks or longer. This does not mean every strategy has been mastered, since improvements are continuous. It does mean that students should be able to work in collaborative groups effectively, recognize the need to struggle with challenging problems, and be well on their way to explaining and recording their thinking.

Initiating the Sequence

Teachers want to begin changing classrooms by allowing students to work with partners in pair-share settings. Early opportunities are brief in duration. Students need to learn how to work with partners as co-learners rather than as leader or follower. To accomplish this, a teacher establishes the rules of pair-share work. As an example, the teacher may assign partners for a set period of time (day or week). The teacher also clearly identifies the expectations for the sharing exercise. The following scenario provides a sample script to assist teachers:

> Class, I think you are capable of learning from one another. Collaborating and sharing ideas and understandings is a lifelong skill you will find very useful. We will start today with brief opportunities for you to talk with a partner. Before you start wondering about a partner, I have already assigned the partner you will work with today. (Teacher pairs up students by proximity to their seating arrangements.)
>
> I am going to spend some time at the beginning of class discussing the mathematics you need to learn today. Then, I will work several example problems for you to observe and ask questions about. At this point in the lesson, I will put a problem on the overhead (or whiteboard) for you to work independently. After you have worked this problem on your own, I will announce, "time." After everyone has stopped working, I will tell you to begin working with your partner. One partner will have 30 seconds to explain what he or she did to work the problem to the other partner. When time is up, I will announce, "switch," and the second partner will share how he or she worked the problem. After 30 seconds, I will announce, "time," and I expect every student to stop talking and look back at me. We will then discuss the problem as a class. (The teacher repeats the signals of "switch" and "time" before assigning the problem.)

In the preceding scenario, following the brief class discussion, the pair-share process is continued with a second problem. The teacher is using this session to train students. At this early stage, thinking and discussions are most likely not going to be rich or deep. Once students have learned the process of sharing, they need to expand their skills. Rather than work independently on a problem, and then share what they did, students need to work with a partner to actually solve the problem together. At this point, students can begin to *explain their thinking and reasoning*. As the National

Council of Teachers of Mathematics (2009) states, "The structure that reasoning brings forms a vital support for understanding and continued learning" (p. 6). Teachers need to encourage students to focus on their thoughts, not just the mathematical procedures used to solve the problem. Two teacher skills emerge, *questioning* and *wait time.*

As students begin talking, teachers need to ask thoughtful questions to probe into student understanding. This requires time for students to think. Wait time is much more effective when students have a partner to talk to about a question. With partners, students are also much more likely to engage in working to solve the question. Without partners, students frequently wait out the process. In a class of 30 students, the odds are individual students will not be called on to answer a question. If the student is called on, the student merely announces that "I don't know," and the teacher usually moves to another student.

As students learn to work with partners and discuss their thinking, more *engaging problems* need to be assigned. Depending on the difficulty of the problem, students may transition into *groups of three or four,* and sustain group work over longer periods of time. Teachers still need classroom signals such as raising their hand, or sounding a small bell, to indicate time for students to become quiet and attentive for additional instructions. Teachers also move around the room to ensure student engagement.

This transition to larger groups and more time requires teachers to hone skills of questions and prompts. Student groups will approach problems in various ways. They also work differently together. Teachers need to help students make sense of mathematics for themselves (National Council of Teachers of Mathematics [NCTM], 2009). Teachers need to be able to ask *questions* that focus students' attention on the problem, and set them on the correct course without giving them answers. Besides asking questions, teachers need to be able to effectively *prompt* groups of students when they are off track or stuck. Teachers may encourage students to "think about yesterday's assignment" or "remember when we converted fractions to decimals." These prompts help students focus on important details but do not have teachers saying, "The answer to that part is 4.3." Students, given the answer, have no motivation to solve the problem, nor do they understand how to get 4.3. Instead of continuing to work, they will most likely wait for teachers to answer another question.

The last element in sequencing strategies is *guiding students to struggle and reason.* Students need to realize that thinking is required to learn mathematics and that struggling to understand or solve problems is natural. Teachers need to help dispel the myth that "if it isn't easy, then I'm no good at math." Students need to learn persistence and resilience. These qualities serve them well in life (Gutierrez, 2000; Organisation for Economic

Co-operation and Development, 2007). Persistence and resilience are learned when students take on and solve difficult problems, both individually and in groups. Challenging problems require students to struggle and grapple with the problem. They must think about the knowledge they have and the information they need and, then, reason what to do. As students engage in these processes, their abilities to articulate their thinking increase. By working with other students, they need to refine and clarify their thought processes and compare their thoughts with the thoughts and ideas expressed by the other members of their group.

As an instructional change journey continues, teachers perfect their knowledge and skills, as do students. Students become adept at working within groups and working independently. Teachers easily transition between different classroom organizations and are flexible in applying these organizations. The listed strategies all continue to be used as needed for the situation. In addition, teachers will find other strategies to incorporate.

Emerging Classroom Conditions

The strategy sequence discussed in the preceding paragraphs offers teachers and leaders a way to transition classrooms from current status to more desired status. This suggested sequence provides time for teachers and students to adjust to new conditions and expectations. The significance of this sequence needs to be highlighted in relation to the desired conditions identified in Chapter 4. As the sequence is introduced and implemented, student thinking is enhanced, encouraged, and clarified. How teachers actually implement these strategies is important. Teachers' attitudes, statements, approaches, responses, and enthusiasm greatly impact the degree to which these strategies will work toward improving the classroom climate.

The strategies, if implemented, will improve student learning. They will also improve students' conscious awareness of their thinking about mathematics. The ultimate goal with these strategies is to directly impact classroom conditions in order to significantly improve student learning. We listed in Figure 4.1 several of these conditions: safe environment, open discussion, metacognition, sense making, self-assessment, time to learn, community of learners, effort over innate ability, and high expectations. The conditions and strategies work together.

As students begin sharing their thinking, and they realize their ideas are respected, a sense of safety increases. This sense of safety promotes more open discussions. As discussions become more open, students are encouraged to explore their thinking and to actually think about their thinking. Being engaged in thinking, students make more sense of the mathematics they are learning. Metacognition, safety, and open discussions provide students a better system for self-assessing their understanding of mathematical concepts and skills.

By working with partners and small groups, students have time to process the content and grasp the significance of learning communities. Learning communities demonstrate to students that everyone has something important to contribute to the learning situation. Through being willing to risk, students find that effort is truly the key to learning, not some "math gene." Finally, as the strategies unfold and the conditions flourish, high expectations emerge. Students gain confidence in their ability to learn and meet any challenge. They begin to want more and expect more from their education and career choices.

THE RELATIONSHIPS AMONG THE STRATEGY SEQUENCE, CONDITIONS, AND GOALS

As stated several times, change begins at the current status and moves forward. Teachers and leaders need to understand current practices and current conditions and desired strategies, conditions, and goals. Successful strategy implementation promotes positive classroom conditions. Positive classroom conditions support reaching desired goals. Goals further the use and addition of effective strategies. Some of the relationships among suggested strategies, positive classroom conditions, and desired goals are presented in the arrangement depicted in Figure 6.2. This organization is not intended to be a comprehensive list. The organization provides some examples of how positive conditions and desired goals are developed and promoted when using the identified strategy. For example, when using the pair-share strategy, teachers are promoting the positive conditions of open discussion and self-assessment. These conditions lead to attaining the desired goals of understanding and meaning, usable knowledge, teaching "with," and problem solving.

Figure 6.2 Relationships Among Recommended Strategies, Conditions, and Outcomes

Recommended Strategy ⟶	Positive Condition ⟶	Desired Goal
Initiating pair-share	Open discussion	Understanding and meaning
		Usable knowledge

Recommended Strategy ⟶	Positive Condition ⟶	Desired Goal
		Teaching "with"
	Self-assessment	Problem solving
Sharing thinking	Safe environment	Teaching "with"
		Guiding
	Open discussion	Understanding and meaning
		Usable knowledge
		Teaching "with"
Questioning and wait time	Time to learn	Active engagement
		Collaboration
Grouping and engaging problem	Community of learners	Collaboration
Using questions and prompts	Self-assessment	Problem solving
Allowing students to struggle	Metacognition	Metacognitive behavior and reflecting
		Explanation of thinking and reasoning
	Sense making	Preexisting knowledge
		Assisting in categorization and finding patterns
		Global network
Encouraging reasoning	Self-assessment	Problem solving

Note: Since an aligned and implemented curriculum is prerequisite and fundamental to successful mathematics teaching and learning, it is not included as a positive condition in this figure.

VISIBLE THINKING SCENARIO 7: BASIC ADDITION AND SUBTRACTION FACTS

After working on basic addition and subtraction facts, the teacher provides students with a game for further practice.

Problem

The game is played by two students. Each pair is given cards with basic addition and subtraction facts, one fact per side. The students shuffle their cards. Each turns a card over and performs the operation indicated to get an answer. The student with the greatest correct number for an answer receives a point. Students are encouraged to use manipulatives to resolve any disagreements in their answers.

Mathematics Within the Problem

The NCTM, in its work *Principles and Standards for School Mathematics* (2000) and its work *Curriculum Focal Points* (2006), as well as the *Common Core State Standards* (2010), all support students being fluent in recalling basic addition and subtraction facts.

What Are Students Doing Incorrectly?

During the time students were playing the game, the teacher was moving about the room listening and observing. He was specifically watching for students who were overly dependent on the use of manipulatives in solving the basic fact problems. He anticipated some students would continue to struggle with facts such as 9 + 7, 17 – 8, and 7 + 6, but he expected students to mentally perform all doubles (1 + 1, 2 + 2, 3 + 3, . . .) as well as some of the traditionally easier facts such as 5 + 3, 6 + 2, and 5 – 3.

During his observation, he detected an unusual amount of conversation with one student pair. He moved in the general direction but stopped at a student pair adjacent to the students of interest. As he listened, he heard the students discussing every answer. One student (B) immediately worked both problems, while the other student (A) was making wild guesses.

What Are Students Thinking and Saying Incorrectly?

The teacher realized he would need to intervene, but he waited a few more minutes in order to gather more information. He noted that it did not seem to matter which number facts were displayed; the one student was unable to answer any of them correctly. Even the usually simple facts like 5 + 0 were being missed. He decided it was time to intervene, and he believed the one student (A) had somehow missed every point during instruction and did not know any of his facts. The teacher reassigned the student getting all facts correct to work with another student whose partner (Student C) was also having some difficulty but nothing to the degree of the first student (A).

Teacher Intervention

The teacher asked the two students who were having difficulty (A and C) to move to a table in the back of the room and play a few rounds of the game while he watched. Student C was able to play the game and mentally calculate most of the facts. Student A was still making wild guesses. On the third hand, the teacher asked Student A to stop and look at his card. The problem was 5 + 4. Student A said the answer was 6 and then quickly said 7. The teacher put five cubes on the desk and asked the student, "How many more do I need to add?" Student A responded, "4," and the teacher asked him to do the addition. Student A responded, "I start with 5, then I add on 6, 7, 8, 9 (pointing at the cubes as he counted)—the answer is 9."

On the next hand, Student A drew the card 7 − 2. Before Student A could answer, the teacher said, "I have 7. How many am I taking away?" Student A responded, "2," and then stated, "7 take away 2 is 5." After continuing to work with Student A, the teacher realized he knew many more facts than the teacher first thought and also knew number conservation. The teacher realized Student A needed some practice on a few of the more difficult facts, but generally he was not out of range with the rest of the class. He realized that when Student A became nervous or stressed, he resorted to guessing.

> ### How did the teacher use visible thinking to effectively intervene?
>
> *By having students work in pairs to practice basic facts, the teacher had time to listen and observe. Because students were talking and sharing, he was able to home in on students who were having difficulty. When he intervened with Student A, he discovered his initial reaction concerning Student A's ability did not reflect reality, and the student's lack of knowledge of the basic facts was not nearly as serious as he first assumed. He also learned that Student A would most likely perform poorly under a "timed facts test." The teacher was able to diagnose Student A's difficulty and appropriately plan for intervention that would work for him.*

VISIBLE THINKING SCENARIO 8: EXPONENTS

Evaluating algebraic expressions containing whole number coefficients and whole number exponents is a benchmark or expectation that now begins in Grade 7 or 8. Both the NCTM *Curriculum Focal Points* (2006) and the *Common Core State Standards* (2010) put the emphasis on exponents in Grade 8. Correctly understanding exponents is necessary as students move toward solving real-world problems involving polynomial expressions.

For some students, however, this task is not as simple as mathematics teachers often believe. Misconceptions abound. One is an order of operations error. For example, the error manifests in the following way: $3x^2 = (3x)^2$. In this scenario, we present a problem where another misconception occurs.

Problem

Evaluate $3x^3 + 4x^2 + x + 2$ when $x = 3$

Mathematics Within the Problem

Exponents are mathematical notations that represent the power of a number. For instance, $10^2 = 10 \times 10$ and $10^3 = 10 \times 10 \times 10$. This notation works for any base such as 2, 3, or 100. For example, we can write $2^3 = 2 \times 2 \times 2$ or $3^4 = 3 \times 3 \times 3 \times 3$.

Students were expected to evaluate the expression by substituting a given value for x and then computing an answer. In the preceding case, $3x^3 + 4x^2 + x + 2$, students were to write $3(3)^3 + 4(3)^2 + (3) + 2$. Simplifying the expression, students should get $3(27) + 4(9) + 5 = 81 + 36 + 5 = 122$.

What Are Students Doing Incorrectly?

The teacher was working with students on evaluating expressions in preparation for solving equations. As she walked around, she observed several students in the class continuing to consider the exponents as factors. This manifests itself in 3^2 being treated as 3×2 rather than 3×3, or 4^3 as 4×3 rather than $4 \times 4 \times 4$.

This error was made more difficult because students often calculated powers correctly when the base was a number rather than a variable. In other words, students would correctly work $3^3 = 3 \times 3 \times 3 = 27$. However, when the context changed to evaluating an algebraic expression at a given value, students resorted to multiplying the value by the exponent to arrive at an answer of 18 (or $9 \times 2 = 18$) rather than by itself to get the correct answer of 81 (or 9×9).

What Are Students Thinking and Saying Incorrectly?

When evaluating the expression $3x^3 + 4x^2 + x + 2$ at $x = 3$, students were correctly writing $3(3)^3 + 4(3)^2 + 3 + 2$. They understood how to approach evaluating algebraic expressions. However, they now simplified by treating 3^3 as 3×3 and ended with $3(9) + 4(6) + 3 + 2 = 27 + 32 + 5 = 64$.

Teacher Intervention

The teacher knew she could not move forward without correcting this misunderstanding and confusion. First, she needed to find out how many students were confused and who the students were. She recalled an inservice session on monitoring student learning by using signaling strategies (Hunter, 2004). As she prepared her lesson for the next day, she selected five multiple-choice problems from the end section in the textbook. She solved the problems using the inaccurate strategy that students were using. She then constructed laminated strips of paper, with red on one side and green on the other.

On the following class day, the teacher handed each student a laminated strip. She wrote one of the problems on the whiteboard with the two answer choices and instructed the students to solve the problem independently.

After a few minutes of work time, she told the students to be ready to show her either the red side or the green side of the laminated strip. She told the students not to signal until she said to do so: red if they thought the answer was A (the correct answer) and green if they thought the answer was B (the incorrect answer). Then, the teacher asked the students to show her their choice.

The teacher scanned the room looking for green sides of the cards. She then assigned the next problem. While the students were working, she made notes to herself. The teacher always used red for A, and green for B, but she changed positions of the correct and incorrect answers. After the five problems, she was confident she knew which students were having difficulty and which ones were not.

Based on the information she had just gathered, the teacher provided a brief explanation about what was occurring concerning evaluating expressions using exponents. She formed the class into pairs so that the students having difficulty were partnered with students who could tutor them. The teacher stressed the importance of being able to correctly evaluate expressions and the need to clearly understand exponential notation since exponents were a critical part of algebra. She allowed students to work several problems together while she moved about the room listening to conversations and asking questions. She decided that she would use evaluating expressions as a warm-up exercise over the next several days.

> ### How was the teacher able to utilize visible thinking to intervene and correct a potentially serious misunderstanding?
>
> *The teacher decided to get immediate feedback from students. Based on these data, she clarified the importance of understanding exponents and assigned peer tutors. She monitored student understanding, stressed the need for students to understand this concept, and arranged to provide additional practice.*

SUMMARY

Teachers, with the help of leaders, can change their classrooms to become more inclusive and successful. Regardless of their current level of strategy usage, improvements—lasting improvements—can be made. By working through a sequence of strategies, whether the list provided in this chapter, one of their own creation, or a combination, teachers can manage positive change.

Change needs to be considered in some form of sequence in which the teacher can envision how the students in the classroom will steadily make progress toward making their thinking more visible to themselves, their classmates, and their teacher. The strategies unfold as the teacher, and students, become more comfortable. One major support beam for visible thinking is in student discussion. For this reason, grouping strategies must be included if change is to occur.

7

How Are Lessons Designed to Achieve Short-Term and Long-Term Changes?

I n Chapter 5, we presented teaching approaches needed for reshaping mathematics classrooms, and in Chapter 6, a sequence for instituting instructional changes. As teachers work to achieve more effective classrooms, they may discover that their current lesson structures and styles no longer serve them well. Even though progress can begin with the current structures, teachers need to transition to the use of a more efficient model.

Making this transition, however, does not mean that one approach is discarded and another adopted but, rather, that another approach is added when it is needed. Teachers and leaders know that one lesson structure, just like only one strategy, is not effective for every mathematics concept to be learned. Effective practitioners in every field have a wealth of tools to select from and use according to the conditions of the situation.

THE CURRENT APPROACH TO TEACHING MATHEMATICS

As pointed out in Chapter 3, research has identified the prominent elements of a usual or typical mathematics lesson in classrooms across the United States: a review of yesterday's lesson and work, introduction of today's lesson with examples provided by the teacher, practice on procedural steps from the illustrated problems, supervised practice, and homework assignment (National Commission on Mathematics and Science Teaching for the 21st Century, 2000). The problem is not that this method of instruction, by itself, is wrong but, rather, that alternative lesson approaches are excluded. There is no balance.

Strategies, Conditions, and Actions That Are Missing

By focusing lessons on one approach, only strategies and actions that fit that approach are ever used. As a result, only students who can learn from these limited strategies are successful. In order to bring more students into the circle of success for mathematics learning, additional strategies need to be used in a balanced manner. Inclusion of additional strategies means different lesson approaches are employed.

In Chapter 4, we provided a list of strategies, conditions, and actions that are recommended for use in mathematics classrooms. This list is repeated here as Figure 7.1. Many of these identified elements are either missing or marginalized by the current approach to teaching mathematics.

Figure 7.1 Categories of Research-Based Instructional Elements		
Strategies	**Conditions**	**Actions**
Interesting, engaging problems	Safe environment	Opportunity to learn
Questioning	Open discussions	Active engagement
Wait time	Aligned curriculum	Enthusiasm
Manipulatives	Implemented curriculum	Challenging work
Vocabulary development	Metacognition	Class participation
Graphic organizers	Sense making	Technology inclusion
Pair-share	Self-assessment	Connections
Working in groups	Time to learn	Transfer of learning
Peer tutoring	Community of learners	Continuous assessment
Journal writing	Effort over innate ability	Feedback
Rubric scoring	High expectations	Variety of strategies

Without most of the research-based, effective strategies and actions being used regularly in mathematics classrooms to create positive conditions, most students are not going to experience success. These missing elements result in students frequently being set up for failure. While clearly every strategy and action is not to be used every day, they should be used regularly. Once achieved, the conditions should be present in mathematics classrooms regardless of the classroom approach selected to teach a daily lesson.

Problems That Arise for Students

Three specific problems occur as a result of the dominant approach to teaching. These problems emphasize the weaknesses of relying on only one approach to teaching—one model:

1. The current approach relies on practice, and practice is often ineffectively used.

2. The method encourages a lack of motivation and engagement by the absence of challenging problems.

3. The model supports a lack of thinking through meaningful talking and writing.

Lack of Effective Practice

While it is true that practice is required for permanent learning, the type of practice students are involved in determines what they learn and how they learn it. As Sousa (2008) states, "Practice may not make perfect, but it does make permanent" (p. 62). The question, of course, is permanent "what"? The practice used during the typical mathematics lesson does not follow the basic research on effective practice. Sousa goes on to warn that "it is very difficult to change a skill that has been practiced and remembered, even if it is not correct" (p. 63). Hunter (2004) recommends that practice should be a short, meaningful amount over a short period of time. Furthermore, practice for learning needs to include both concentrated and distributed practice to be effective.

Even if done correctly, and students effectively practice a skill, they are only learning one skill. While it is important to learn skills, isolated bits of learned information do not serve problem solving adequately. Isolated skills learned independently do not help students build the neural connections needed to effectively retrieve and transfer the information or skill into new situations.

Lack of Motivation and Engagement

In order to learn, students need some form of motivation. Often, the motivational influences are from the students' family unit or perhaps from their previous levels of success. According to Hunter (2004), there are six factors that directly impact students' motivation: level of concern, feeling tone, success, interest, knowledge of results, and intrinsic and extrinsic motivation. With only rare exception, teachers have control over these factors. Teachers, by the learning activities they plan and present, greatly influence the level of students' motivation.

Motivation and engagement begin with challenging work. Problems that offer a challenge to students are shown to promote greater interest and enjoyment. Students learn best when they are presented with academically challenging work. The challenging work must focus on sense making, problem solving, and skill building (National Research Council [NRC], 2001, 2004).

These motivational factors are not present to any degree in the typical approach to teaching mathematics. For the identified motivational factors to arise in classrooms, additional approaches to teaching are needed. These approaches need to be interesting and to actively engage students. "Research in learning shows that students become cognitively engaged when they are asked to wrestle with new concepts, when they are pushed to understand—for example, by being required to explain their reasoning, defend their conclusions, or explore alternative strategies and solutions" (NRC, 2004, p. 49).

Lack of Thinking and Writing

In Chapter 3, we declared that students are not being asked to think in mathematics classrooms. Using the typical instructional approach, including thinking is difficult since the approach focuses on procedural practice. Thinking comes from a different approach. Students "need the kinds of learning activities that will help them talk, write, and think about the subject matter. By talking and listening to each other's thinking, learners gain the vocabulary, syntax, and rhetoric—the discourses—needed to understand and describe the knowledge structures associated with specific subjects and specific problems (NRC, 2001, p. 26).

These problems are overcome, or at least greatly reduced, when teachers have more than one lesson approach to use in planning and presenting lessons. If students need practice, or demonstration on procedures, the typical approach serves well. The single approach cannot serve well when students need to be challenged, highly engaged, thinking, talking, reasoning, and explaining.

ELEMENTS OF AN ALTERNATIVE INSTRUCTIONAL MODEL

Students learn mathematics in different ways for different reasons. There is no question that every student can learn mathematics (National Council of Teachers of Mathematics [NCTM], 2000) but only when mathematics is presented in a way that provides meaning and makes sense to students (NRC, 2005). In extending these points of view, the NCTM (2009) states, "Mathematical reasoning and sense making are both important outcomes of mathematics instruction, as well as important means by which students come to know mathematics" (p. 12). Meaning and sense making, as well as the other strategies, conditions, and actions listed in Figure 7.1, require different ways of approaching instruction.

Lesson Organization

The structure for a different model for teaching mathematics has three phases: *setting the stage, exploring*, and *summarizing*. The three phases flow one to the next, with each forming a link in the learning chain. Phases do not have specific time durations such as 15 minutes. Time allotted to each phase is determined by the teacher and based on the purpose of the lesson. In some way, each phase is addressed every day, but a lesson incorporating these phases may last several days or a week. This approach is based on students working in groups.

As an example of one way the model may work, suppose a mathematics lesson is designed to cover three class days of instruction (sample lessons are provided in Chapters 8, 9, and 10). On the first day, setting the stage will most likely take longer than the other two phases. After a teacher provides information to students, establishes clear expectations, and forms groups, the exploring phase is launched. For Day 1, exploring may include students gathering important information and generating several "plans of action." The teacher uses the summarizing phase to ensure students have formulated some viable strategies and to ensure that students understand the problem situation to be solved.

In Day 2 of the lesson, setting the stage is short in duration. The teacher stresses key points, ensures students understand their task, and then allows students to engage in exploring. During this phase, students are gathering data, discussing ideas, drawing on their previous learning, formulating various approaches, and organizing their findings. This may be a significant amount of the instructional time. The teacher is moving around helping different student groups. Students are completing the tasks. Summarizing for Day 2 may include students sharing what they are doing to solve the problem as well as some of their challenges.

In Day 3, setting the stage may include a statement of expectations by the teacher as to what the students are preparing to do. The teacher may reinforce that every student is expected to understand what the group has accomplished. Exploring is time for students to affirm their solutions and prepare a way to present and show their findings. Summarizing uses the bulk of instructional time as students share and explain their reasoning, justify their answers, and compare their work with other students' work. The teacher stresses the important mathematics concepts and helps students make connections.

In this model, the entire three-day lesson revolves around setting the stage, exploring, and summarizing, but the length of time devoted to each phase is adjusted according to need and purpose. In other words, this approach is flexible. Teachers and leaders should not see it as prescriptive. Each strategy, condition, and action fits in one or more of the phases within this model. Teachers who are required to state the learning objective every day will have no problem including the requirement within setting the stage. Teachers who wish to periodically lecture, or have students practice specific skills, may select either setting the stage or summarizing as an appropriate place for such activities.

Purposes of the Phases

Setting the Stage

Setting the stage is intended to interest, engage, and motivate students to participate in the mathematics lesson. This phase provides students pertinent information they may need, as well as emphasizing previous mathematics lessons and content they may need. The phase may also be used for teachers to quickly assess student knowledge of previous learning. If the challenging problem to be presented to students requires converting decimals to fractions, teachers may want to know what students recall about this skill.

Setting the stage is a balancing act. Teachers do not want to work the problem for students. If teachers work the problem, then there is no reason for students to work the problem again. Teachers do want to provide just the right amount of information. Teachers need to also remember that this phase occurs every day, so information may be meted out as needed.

Exploring

Exploring is a phase devoted to students. This is the time for students to struggle, think, reason, explain, research, try and fail, and try again. It is a phase where students learn to truly problem solve and to rely on their fellow students. Ideas must be shared. Communication is a vital skill. Students work together to arrange their data, seek patterns, devise and test solutions, and then explain the entire process.

Exploring calls on teachers to perfect their questioning skills. Teachers need to keep students interested and engaged during the process by asking pertinent questions, providing prompts, or offering hints. The question, prompt, or hint must put students back on the right track without providing them an answer. There is a huge difference between a teacher asking, "Have you considered using fractions instead of decimals?" and stating, "The answer for this part is 3/4."

Summarizing

In using this alternative instructional model, summarizing is, perhaps, the most underused phase in mathematics classrooms, but it is so very important. Students need to formalize their learning. They need to engage their brains and discover how components fit together. They learn the mathematics. The summarizing phase ensures students understand the mathematics they have been using. Regardless of the approach they used to solve the problem, they will discover that other groups approached and solved it differently. Students need to understand the relationships between their approach and the other students' approaches.

Even if students solved a problem incorrectly, if they have explored the problem, they have the foundation to understand what went wrong and to self-correct. Since teachers are constantly monitoring, this should not happen often, but it can happen. More likely to occur is that students will have solved the problem using an elementary approach and, as a result, have a poor conceptual understanding of the mathematics. Having explored the problem, and solved the problem, they are better prepared to understand a more in-depth explanation and demonstration.

Listening to students summarize their thinking gives teachers greater insights into what students are understanding and learning. Summarizing thinking requires more than reciting procedures ("I multiplied 13 times 4, put down the 2, and carried the 1 . . ."). Summarizing thinking has students state how they knew what to do. ("I knew that the farmer had 13 baskets and each basket had 4 eggs. I took 10 baskets with 4 eggs, and I know that is 40 eggs. Now, I have 3 baskets with 4 eggs each, so I multiplied 3 times 4 and got 12 eggs. I added 40 eggs and 12 eggs and found out the farmer had 52 eggs.")

Summarizing is also a time for formal assessments as well as short quizzes. If students are working on a project that will be scored using a rubric, the summarizing phase occurs when they complete the project.

Even though students work in groups, assessments can be individual. As a note, formative assessments are ongoing through all three phases. Teachers are continually gathering information about student learning.

TYPES OF PROBLEMS

There are three types of problems that help teachers both shift their thinking about student engagement and transition from their current instructional approach to our recommended model. These problem types can change how classrooms operate. With challenging problems, students need to work in grouping (pairs, threes, or fours) situations. The students need to talk and have sufficient time to correctly solve problems. They also need to share their work since they are proud of their accomplishments.

For their part, teachers need to listen carefully to the students. They must allow students to complete their thoughts without interrupting in order to better understand what students are thinking and to gain insight into students' conceptual knowledge. By changing the types of problems offered in mathematics classrooms, strategies, conditions, and actions follow.

These three problem types are *brainteaser, group worthy*, and *transformed*. (Grade-appropriate problems for each problem type are provided in Chapters 8, 9, and 10.) The problem types serve different needs for students. Teachers should understand the importance and purpose for each type. They also need to correctly identify the mathematics involved in the problem and, then, be prepared to expand their thinking as students devise unique solutions.

Brainteaser Problems

Various dictionary definitions of brainteaser suggest that it is a complex problem requiring careful thought in order to solve it. Brainteaser-type problems are not tricks but, rather, problems that can be solved using logic and reason. These types of problems challenge students to look at mathematics in a very different way than they are accustomed. This is one of the purposes of brainteaser problems. The idea of a brainteaser is to interest and challenge students in a way that is outside the usual routine followed in mathematics classrooms.

This routine is learned by students—how they are to behave and act in mathematics classrooms. They soon discover whether they are "good" at mathematics or "bad." These assessments of self are very powerful, and they influence students' willingness to try. If the students are convinced they are not good in mathematics, then why try to do mathematics?

Brainteaser problems help to break this circular thinking. The situations are unique and interesting. Often, thinking outside of the prescriptive, procedural routines is needed to solve the problem. In addition, brainteaser problems should have multiple solution paths at different levels of difficulty, so all students participate.

Brainteaser problems use mathematics, but these types of problems are often difficult to directly tie to specific mathematics content. Students can use many ways to solve the problem, so teachers need to be able to pull out the mathematics they wish students to focus on. In doing so, teachers must never give students the idea that one way of solving the problem is correct or better and another way is incorrect or worse.

Group-Worthy Problems

Group-worthy problems (Boaler, 2006) are content based and content specific even though students will be drawing from a wide variety of mathematics skills. The problems lend themselves to multiple paths for reaching a solution. As the name suggests, students work collaboratively to solve the problems.

Level of difficulty is an important factor in group-worthy problems. If the problem is too easy, students are bored and end up either not working or working independently. If the problem is too difficult, then combined knowledge is insufficient, and students become frustrated.

Transformed Problems

These problems are most like traditional problems. They are usually based on multiple-choice format problems, but they have been "transformed" into more open-ended type problems. The answer choices have been removed and the problem restated in such a way that students can think and reason, often starting by offering an opinion. With answer choices removed, students must spend more time thinking about and discussing the problem.

Transformed problems lend themselves very well to student pairs. Transformed problems frequently wind their way back around to the point where students are ready to correctly solve a related traditional problem independently.

SUMMARY

The typical approach to teaching mathematics is fraught with problems when it is used exclusively. Students, at a very early age, begin to accept that they are not able to learn mathematics. A natural response to this belief is to give up or quit trying. When students quit trying, teachers perceive the students as unmotivated and not caring. The cycle is now complete, and continues to rotate for the rest of the students' educational career, unless some serious intervention occurs.

Sadly, if the intervention uses the same typical approach, what chance does the student have of suddenly "getting" mathematics? Students need a variety of instructional strategies to learn mathematics, and these various strategies must start at Day 1. Students need to practice skills and learn procedural fluency, but this is only a small fraction of learning mathematics. Student thinking needs to be cultivated, nurtured, and encouraged. Students must be made aware of their thinking and encouraged to openly share. Teachers must seek ways to have students' thinking become visible so they can guide students along the path of conceptual learning.

Part III

Implementing the Alternative Model at Different Grade Levels

8 How Is Thinking Made Visible in Grades K–2 Mathematics?

Teachers in the early elementary grades have the power to awaken the joy of learning mathematics in their students. Brainteaser, group-worthy, and transformed problems, previously explained in Chapter 7, can greatly influence a student's love for problem solving and critical thinking. Furthermore, some educators claim that almost all elementary mathematical skills and concepts can be taught through problem solving (Grouws & Cebulla, 2000). Chapters 8, 9, and 10 provide problems that can be used in teaching three of the most essential concepts elementary students need to know, that is, number sense, fractions, and estimation.

In Grades K through 2, one of the first big ideas or focus points important to learning mathematics includes developing number sense skills (*Common Core State Standards*, 2010; National Council of Teachers of Mathematics, 2006). Number sense is often described as an intuitive understanding of numbers, their magnitude, relationships, and how they are affected by operations. A rich understanding of number sense allows students to solve problems that are not solved by traditional methods. During preschool, students begin developing the number sense needed to process and manipulate numbers. In Grades K through 2, students begin learning estimation concepts and are exposed to a variety of math problem solving requiring addition and subtraction operations. Examples of brainteaser, group-worthy, and transformed problems for K–2 students follow.

BRAINTEASER PROBLEM EXAMPLE

Problem

A farmer has 3 cows and 2 chickens in her field. Help the farmer find the number of legs and tails for her cows and chickens.

Mathematics Within the Problem

Appropriate for first grade, this problem is typically described as a brainteaser process problem. Students at this level do not know, and are not expected to know, the algorithms of multiplication and addition with regrouping. The algorithms are doable on a concrete basis but are not yet part of their symbolic manipulation strategies, either mentally or with paper and pencil. To solve the problem, many students may draw pictures of three cows and two chickens and simply count the tails and legs. (It is assumed that the tail feathers of a chicken at this primary grade level are tails. This is not a trick question.)

Setting the Stage

The teacher sets the stage by telling the problem solving situation as a story:

On my way to school this morning, I met a farmer whose cows and chickens were in a field across the highway. The farmer did not want to cross the busy highway but needed to know the total number of legs and tails of her cows and chickens. I told her I thought we could help her if she knew how many cows and how many chickens she had in the field across the highway. "Well," she said, "there are 3 cows and 2 chickens in that field." Will you work with a partner and find the total number of legs and tails for the farmer? When you are finished, I want each partner pair to show the rest of us how you found your answer.

The teacher assigns partners and encourages the students to begin working on the problem.

Exploring

The teacher provides time for the children to work on the problem. Without specific directions, many of the students draw pictures of cows and chickens and begin counting the tails and legs. Some students use manipulatives to model the cows and chickens, and then count. However, one pair of children presents a different approach. Their exact explanation during this exploring phase is recorded as follows:

> We did not need to draw 3 cows. One cow 3 times would be enough. Then we saw we just needed the legs and tails, so that is what we did for the chicken. There were 15 legs and tails for the cows and 6 legs and tails for the chickens. We know that 5 more than 15 is 20 and 6 is 1 more than 5, so 1 more than 20 is 21.

Summarizing

The teacher encourages students to share with the whole class their solutions to the problem. The teacher helps students compare and contrast their ideas.

Formative Assessment of Visible Thinking

During the exploring time, the teacher moves about the room listening in on students' thinking. The teacher is able to view students' depictions of the problem. The teacher asks probing and clarifying questions to individual students and student pairs. By doing this, the teacher determines what concepts students actually understand and what learning still needs to occur. Formative assessment of visible thinking provides evidence that students are being challenged and applying previously learned knowledge.

Connections to Strategies, Actions, and Conditions

With challenging and interesting problems that students work on in pairs, teachers can ask probing questions with appropriate wait time. A teacher may ask questions of one group, move on to another group, and then return to the first group for students' explanations.

By selecting problems that have multiple solution approaches, teachers are able to gather continuous assessment data. The data are used to provide appropriate and immediate feedback to students. Stories allow teachers to display excitement and enthusiasm for mathematics and to encourage class participation. They also provide a simple illustration of how mathematics and literature might connect.

Students need to be encouraged to think about mathematics from the beginning of their formal education. By using brainteaser-style problems, teachers are able to encourage students to express their ideas and thoughts without fear of ridicule. Students use the tools at their disposal, so they are able to make sense of the situation. When observing and discussing other students' thoughts and solutions, they are able to self-assess their thinking.

GROUP-WORTHY PROBLEM EXAMPLE

Problem

Students need to practice adding in order to become fluent in the procedure. Practicing by completing worksheets soon grows tedious, and students quickly stop caring if they get the correct answer or not. Their goal becomes "finishing the worksheet." Problems such as the "sums" one that follows provide multiple opportunities for students to practice addition, while also being challenged. The problem is identified in Figure 8.1, and progresses through various iterations. Reasoning also becomes an important focus as students find different solutions.

Figure 8.1 Can You Find a Pattern? Sums Around Sums

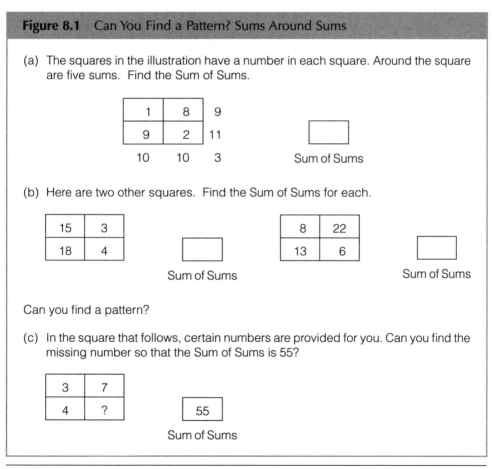

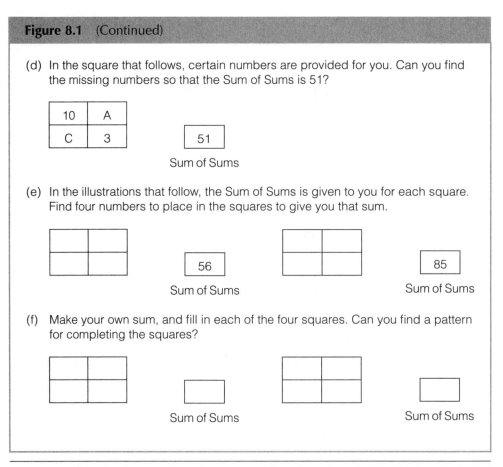

Figure 8.1 (Continued)

(d) In the square that follows, certain numbers are provided for you. Can you find the missing numbers so that the Sum of Sums is 51?

10	A
C	3

51

Sum of Sums

(e) In the illustrations that follow, the Sum of Sums is given to you for each square. Find four numbers to place in the squares to give you that sum.

56

Sum of Sums

85

Sum of Sums

(f) Make your own sum, and fill in each of the four squares. Can you find a pattern for completing the squares?

Sum of Sums

Sum of Sums

Mathematics Within the Problem

These problems have multiple answers, so all students would not necessarily get the same answers. Students will most likely solve the problems by trial and error. They should soon begin realizing that the sums need to add to the identified sum. This understanding reduces the number of random guesses.

Reasoning about the five sums helps students find solutions. In problem (c), three numbers, 3, 7, and 4, are provided in the grid. The Sum of Sums is 55. With this information, students can find two of the five sums: $3 + 7 = 10$ and $3 + 4 = 7$. Subtracting $10 + 7 = 17$ from 55 leaves a difference of 38. What does this represent? It is $(7 + ?) + (3 + ?) + (4 + ?)$. So $38 - 7 - 3 - 4 = 24 = ? + ? + ?$, or the missing number is 8.

In problem (d) with a Sum of Sums equal to 51 and two numbers, 10 and 3, provided, students might add 10 + 3 = 13 and then subtract 13 from 51. Now, the remaining sum is 51 − 13 = 38. The number 10 is added twice in the remaining Sum of Sums. Likewise, the number 3 is added twice. So subtracting 6 and 20 from 38 gives 12. What does this represent? It represents twice the first missing value A and twice the second missing value C. That means that the sum of the two numbers must be 6. Possible solutions are shown in Figure 8.2.

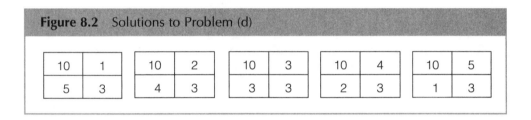

Figure 8.2 Solutions to Problem (d)

As suggested, trial and error will be a preferred method for solving Sum of Sums problems for the grade levels we are targeting. Mathematically, however, solutions can be found using algebra. By labeling the squares a, b, c, and d, the sum is given by $3a + 2b + 2c + 3d = 3(a + d) + 2(b + c)$ or $3x + 2y$.

If the Sum of Sums is 56, then $3x + 2y = 56$. Then x could be 12 and y would be 10. So pick two numbers that add to 12 and two numbers that add to 10. Place them in the squares and they work. The value of x could be 10; then y would be 13. Selecting two numbers that have a sum of 10 and two numbers that have a sum of 13 also provides a solution.

This transforms column addition into a problem solving mode along with continual practice on multiplace addition. For other grade levels, fractions and integers can be used.

Setting the Stage

A teacher will want to demonstrate a problem by providing a grid with the squares completed. The teacher then shows students the sums and then the Sum of Sums. Next, the teacher shows students a problem with some of the numbers missing. The teacher asks students to think about how they might approach solving the problem and finding the missing numbers. Students offer various ideas and suggestions. The teacher then lets students work to finish the problem. After students have worked on the problem, the teacher checks to see what students have discovered. The teacher then assigns similar problems to student groups of two or three.

Exploring

The teacher moves about the room listening to students and observing their work. As students reach a comfort level of solving certain problem types, the teacher may provide the student groups with more challenging problems.

Summarizing

The teacher selects certain groups to place their problem solutions on the whiteboard or overhead. Students explain their thinking and solutions to the class.

Formative Assessment of Visible Thinking

While the problems are interesting and challenging, their use enables the teacher to evaluate students' computational fluency. How are students using trial-and-error approaches? When students are adding to find sums, how quickly are they able to do so?

Connections to Strategies, Actions, and Conditions

An advantage of these Sum of Sums problems is the opportunity for students to think and reason at various levels of ability. Teachers are able to address diverse student needs by regulating which problems are provided. Students are able to practice critical skills while solving problems that prove interesting even at the lowest levels.

TRANSFORMING PROBLEM EXAMPLE

Problem

Students are expected to compare and order two-digit numbers. The order can be from least to greatest or from greatest to least. Problems assigned to students usually resemble the following examples:

1. Which number is greatest?

A. 19   B. 72   C. 23   D. 58

2. Which set of numbers is in order from least to greatest?

A.	15	51	37	85
B.	86	73	92	41
C.	22	35	49	71*
D.	11	64	38	59

Problems like the preceding ones are important, but students soon grow weary of repeating the same exercises. Students need to be active. Being able to move around the room, or even outside, greatly reduces fatigue and maintains interest.

Teachers have several options for having students practice comparing and ordering numbers. First, teachers may create a deck of numeral cards from 0 to 99. One card is given to each student, and as the teacher calls on individuals, the students line up in the proper order around the interior of the classroom. Students may get in order according to the students already called, or the teacher may have students estimate where they might be located in the room and then adjust as other students are added.

Second, teachers can have students work in groups of four or five. Each student draws a card, and the students arrange themselves in order. One student from the group should explain how the numbers are arranged and why the order is correct. Students take turns in this role.

Mathematics Within the Problem

Students are expected to understand the significance of place value. When working with two-digit numbers, the digit in the 10s place determines the magnitude unless two numbers have the same 10s digit. In most cases, students are able to sequence numbers according to the digit in the 10s place. Teachers need to decide when to introduce students to the concept of ordering numbers when the 10s digits are the same. Students should be able to correctly sequence numbers from 0 to 100.

Setting the Stage

A teacher may decide which variation of the sequencing game to have students play. Based on this decision, students are provided with the appropriate materials—either the teacher has a deck of number cards or each group of four students has a set. Teachers may decide to play the game with the entire class as a means of reviewing place value and comparing, or they may decide to select four students to come to the front of the room to demonstrate the activity.

Exploring

During this phase, students play the game in groups.

Summarizing

The teacher has each group take turns explaining why the order within their group is correct. Students would say something like, "Our numbers are 32, 54, 75, and 84. We have them in order from least to greatest. We did this by looking at the 10s place. We know that 30 is less than 50. Both 30 and 50 are less than 70. And 30, 50, and 70 are less than 80." The teacher will want to emphasize the importance of the 10s place.

Formative Assessment of Visible Thinking

Teachers are certainly watching and listening. In this case, teachers may want to have some form of written documentation to further analyze student understanding. They may have students draw four cards, write down the numbers on the cards, and then place the numbers in order, either greatest to least or least to greatest. Students then turn their work in to the teacher. As an alternative version, the teacher may decide to write four numbers on the whiteboard or overhead in random order. All students are asked to write the same numbers in the correct order on their papers.

Connections to Strategies, Actions, and Conditions

Students are highly engaged when allowed to move. By working in groups, any errors or misunderstandings are usually corrected immediately. Students are engaged because they are active and taking turns. Students physically move, verbally state, and hear both the order and the explanation numerous times. These actions build number relationships and understandings.

SUMMARY

Number sense and computation are two big-picture ideas for students to master at the early elementary level. These concepts can be taught through problem solving experiences. Making student thinking visible at the elementary level focuses on investigations and understanding of mathematical content. Students are encouraged and allowed to share their strategies and their processes with one another. Models, manipulatives, and drawings can be used by students to make sense of the mathematics they are learning. Teachers can quickly assess strengths and weaknesses by making student thinking visible.

9 How Is Thinking Made Visible in Grades 3–5 Mathematics?

Students in Grades 3 through 5 are solidifying their proficiency with addition and subtraction as well as soundly developing the concepts of multiplication and division. Both the National Council of Teachers of Mathematics *Curriculum Focal Points* (2006) and the *Common Core State Standards* (2010) stress these critical concepts, as well as the concept of fractions. Fraction recognition is not difficult for elementary students; however, operations with fractions are hard for most children. Addition, subtraction, multiplication, and division of fractions are often taught abstractly as rules. These procedural rules make little sense to students and are easily forgotten.

A third focus point important for elementary mathematics and beyond is computational estimation in problem solving. Estimations are approximations for exact numbers and are often confused by elementary students with the idea of merely guessing. Strategies needed in problem solving start developing in preschool as children begin learning the base 10 numeration system. Children in Grades 3 through 5 acquire specific computational estimation strategies such as front-end estimation with adjustment; friendly, special numbers; compatible numbers; rounding; and clustering—all necessary to solve real-world problems.

BRAINTEASER PROBLEM EXAMPLE

Students receive a great deal of practice in multi-digit column addition as well as multi-digit subtraction, similar to the examples that follow:

$$
\begin{array}{r}
3{,}734 \\
81 \\
209 \\
+3{,}485 \\
\hline
\end{array}
\qquad
\begin{array}{r}
93{,}742 \\
-\ 6{,}523 \\
\hline
\end{array}
$$

Problem

Teachers are seeking ways to encourage students to engage in addition and subtraction practice. The preceding problems can be easily transformed into problems that add greater interest and challenge, require thinking and reasoning, and still achieve the required practice. These brainteaser problems have some of the digits removed and replaced by question marks (?):

$$
\begin{array}{r}
?{,}734 \\
8? \\
209 \\
+\ 3{,}?85 \\
\hline
?1{,}1?7 \\
\end{array}
\qquad
\begin{array}{r}
93{,}742 \\
-\ 6{,}523 \\
\hline
?7{,}?19 \\
\end{array}
$$

Students are asked to complete the problem by solving for the question marks (?).

Mathematics Within the Problem

Addition and subtraction are basic fluency skills for students in first and second grade. Continuing on in third grade through fifth grade, students are now comfortable with basic facts and regrouping strategies; however, they need to practice these skills. Students are provided ample time to practice the skills of addition and subtraction in problems identified in the preceding paragraphs.

Setting the Stage

Teachers want to encourage student participation by creating a story for the addition problem:

I have been thinking about going on a vacation this summer to different locations in the world. I'm not sure where I want to go, so I've been collecting some data about different possibilities. I recorded the distances between the different locations. I wrote the distances in pencil. Yesterday, I found my list of distances, but the paper got wet, and I couldn't read all the numbers. Can you help me figure out how far I was thinking about traveling and whether you think I can get to all the places?

For the subtraction problem, the teacher may describe the following situation:

> The other day, I heard that attendance at the Super Bowl was down from last year. I tried to write down all the numbers, but I didn't write fast enough. Can you help me find out the attendance at the Super Bowl?

Exploring

The teacher provides time for students to work on the assigned problems. The teacher may provide several problems for students to work by stating they have different route possibilities or different Super Bowl years of attendance. Students may work independently or with partners.

Summarizing

The teacher wants to have students explain their reasoning. With these types of problems, students need to say more than just the operation they performed. For instance, in the ones column in the addition problem, students need to state that they needed to combine 4, 9, 5, and some number that would produce a 7 in the ones column answer. Students might state: "If I add 4 + 9 + 5, I get 18, so I must add on 9 more to reach 27."

The teacher also has an opportunity to discuss reasonableness of answers. Once the problems are solved, the teacher can discuss various trip possibilities with the anticipated amount of travel, based on the answer to the addition problem.

Formative Assessment of Visible Thinking

Students can be provided with "digit" cards from 0 to 9. The teacher writes a multiplace subtraction problem such as the following:

$$
\begin{array}{r}
6,?5? \\
- 4,397 \\
\hline
?,8?6
\end{array}
$$

Using the digit cards, students determine the missing digits in the problem. As the students are working, the teacher is moving about the room listening to students or observing their work.

Connections to Strategies, Actions, and Conditions

By using different problems with a unique twist, teachers can encourage greater interest and participation from students. In this situation, some students may work independently, while others may work with partners. Provided this option, students may feel safer in offering answers. These brainteaser problems increase student awareness of the relationship between addition and subtraction.

GROUP-WORTHY PROBLEM EXAMPLE

Problem

> Mrs. Smith has 2 and 1/3 pizzas left over from her school class party. She will take home the leftover pizza for her family to eat for dinner. If there are 4 members in her family, how much pizza will she be able to serve to each member?

Mathematics Within the Problem

At the Grade 5 level, most students do not know how to divide fractions as a pencil-and-paper skill. This problem allows students to partition each pizza into fourths and also equally divide the remaining one third of a pizza.

This experience provides students an opportunity to informally explore mixed numerals before learning a formal process. This understanding is very important for students since once an algorithm is presented, students often forget about the solution making sense. Informally, students have little difficulty dividing 2 pizzas evenly among 4 people. Students generally use fourths for each pizza and then share out the pieces (even though they could divide each pizza in half). Students would know that each person would get two of the 1/4 pizzas.

However, once the problem becomes 2 1/3, students tend to become quickly confused and fail to think about the situation being 2 pizzas and 1/3 of a pizza. They forget about reasonableness and merely try to perform some manner of calculation. Experiences like the problem offered provide teachers an opportunity to assist students in estimating reasonable solutions before performing calculations.

Setting the Stage

Teachers should remind fifth graders that fractional parts are equal shares of a whole. Basic fraction recognition begins in kindergarten and first grade. Generally, students learn to add and subtract like fractions in Grades 3 and 4. At the fifth grade level, students are introduced to multiplication of fractions. Equal sharing with division of fractions using math models and manipulatives may also be an introductory skill; however, the algorithm for division of fractions is not a secure, mastery skill for fifth graders.

Students are provided with a copy of the problem. Placing the problem on a projection device or whiteboard, the teacher verbally reads the problem out loud.

Exploring

Students are provided a few minutes to think about the problem and make a drawing of the situation. They are encouraged to think about what needs to happen to solve the problem rather than to actually solve it. Students are then assigned partners and asked to meet with their partners to discuss their drawings and thoughts.

At this point, students should be able to work in partner pairs to solve this fraction problem and should be allowed to use plastic or paper fraction circle pieces or sketch fraction circles on paper to represent 2 pizzas. Instead of merely following a rule or a procedure that was presented, students will be visualizing fractions and dividing without knowingly applying any given rule. Students should be encouraged to use the guess-and-check strategy to determine the number of pieces. However, by using teacher-made or commercially available fraction circles, students can take the $1/3$ fraction piece and place four other congruent fraction pieces on top of it until they find a match. In this case, four of the $1/12$ fraction pieces will cover the $1/3$ fraction piece. Therefore, each family member would receive $1/2$ of a pizza and $1/12$ of a pizza. Now, however, what are these fractional amounts in terms of one pizza? That is, what is $1/2 + 1/12$? In a similar fashion, students cover the $1/2$ piece with $1/12$ pieces, noting that 6 of them cover the $1/2$ piece. Their result: $6/12 + 1/12 = 7/12$.

Summarizing

This fraction visible thinking activity is more of a learning activity versus an assignment or homework. The students learn so much from each other's thinking. Some students may not believe that $1/3$ can be divided by $1/4$ without a hands-on experience.

With this idea of a learning activity in mind, the teacher should encourage students to articulate their solutions. The teacher wants students to discuss their thinking about how they approached the problem, and what they knew needed to be done, more than their procedural steps.

After group discussion, the teacher could have students describe and record their thinking in a journal. Students need time to reflect on their understanding and opportunities to express their thoughts.

Formative Assessment of Visible Thinking

While moving about the room, the teacher can accurately assess students' conceptual understanding of division of fractions. As students externalize their thoughts by sharing with one another how they solved the problem, the teacher can observe misconceptions and degrees of understanding.

Connections to Strategies, Actions, and Conditions

There are a variety of strategies that may be used with group-worthy problems. Questioning and wait time are used during both exploration and summarization. Manipulatives are used. With journal recording, teachers can use rubric scoring of students' written explanations if desired.

For actions, using this problem type encourages students to make connections with previous learning and understandings. Students are actively engaged because they are given the opportunity to work together. These informal solutions with manipulatives serve to strengthen transfer of learning to new, but related, situations.

Through exploring these types of problems, effective classroom conditions are promoted. Students learn to express their thoughts in a safe, supportive environment. They realize that mathematics makes sense, and it is not just a set of rules and procedures to be memorized. Students experience working in a collaborative environment and realize the classroom functions as a community of learners.

TRANSFORMING PROBLEM EXAMPLE

Problem

Your school principal has enough perfect-attendance certificates to give to 350 students. The following number of students in each grade level has perfect attendance:

Grade 1: 102   Grade 2: 127   Grade 3: 165   Grade 4: 139

Does the principal have enough certificates for all of them, or do more certificates need to be purchased? Use front-end estimation to determine your estimated answer.

Mathematics Within the Problem

This Grade 3 or 4 problem focuses on the strategy of front-end estimation with compensation. For students, computational estimation is being able to quickly and easily get a number that is close enough to the exact answer of the problem without taking the time to use pencil-and-paper addition.

Front-end estimation involves a simplified mental calculation. To estimate the answer to the problem, use only the left-most digit (100s place) of the numbers being estimated.

Add 1 + 1 + 1 + 1 (100 + 100 + 100 + 100 = 400). This shows that at least 400 certificates will be needed.

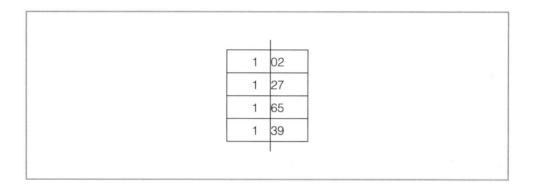

This strategy is often used when adding or multiplying; however, an underestimate will probably occur. Front-end estimation is not as accurate as rounding but is useful for a quick initial estimate.

Compensation is used after the initial estimate is made; however, the estimator must decide if this first estimate is too big or too small. The front-end estimate may need to be altered depending on how far off the initial estimate is. The amount that it is over or under is then estimated with a strategy involving *compensation* and *compatible numbers,* which will be used to update the initial estimate.

To use compatible numbers, make the problem easier by stating: 2 + 27 + 65 is about another 100 + 39 (taken from 1_02_, 1_27_, 1_65_, and 1_39_). So 140 is a reasonable estimate. The initial estimate of 400 plus 140 is well over 500. Therefore, the principal will not have enough perfect-attendance certificates.

Setting the Stage

Students should be allowed to work together in partner pairs or a group of three or four students. More than likely, the strategy of front-end estimation has been taught through direct instruction. Now it is time for students to apply the strategy in a problem solving situation.

Exploring

As students are given the problem to solve, the teacher may want to ask the third or fourth graders to dialogue with their partners about the problem itself. As students determine the problem situation and work toward a solution, the teacher should move about the room providing some guidance as needed.

Summarizing

The teacher should have students discuss their thinking about this problem as they want to ensure students do not merely add the numbers. Estimation is an invaluable skill in mathematics that must be taught and practiced.

Formative Assessment of Visible Thinking

When students interact with others in cooperative problem solving and share their thinking out loud, teachers are able to help identify misunderstandings. Students not only profit from solving a problem; they receive the most benefit from explaining their thinking and helping others. Brain-based learning research indicates this greatly increases content retention as well as boosting student confidence.

Connections to Strategies, Actions, and Conditions

The primary action teachers are seeking is transfer of learning. Students need to increase number sense and awareness through estimating. These skills remind students that mathematics makes sense. Using the strategy of working with pairs or partners, teachers can encourage the actions of participation and engagement. Estimation problems and group discussions promote the classroom conditions of student self-assessment and metacognition.

SUMMARY

The problems in this Chapter focus on the basic operations of addition, subtraction, multiplication, and division, as well as the concept of fractions. These topics are big areas of study for students in Grades 3 through 5. While fraction recognition is not usually a difficult skill for elementary students, operations with fractions are. Operations on fractions are frequently taught as abstract rules. Procedural rules without concrete experiences as a foundation make little sense to students. As a result, the rules are easily forgotten, misremembered, or confused. When teachers engage students in activities that make thinking visible in classrooms, concepts are appropriately developed.

10

How Is Thinking Made Visible in Grades 6–8 Mathematics?

The concepts developed in middle school grades, usually Grades 6, 7, and 8, are grounded in operations with rational numbers. These operations are deeper than just computation. Students need to understand fractions, decimals, and percentages since these concepts emerge during algebraic thinking and reasoning. They need to move fluently between and among the various representations. The National Council of Teachers of Mathematics, in *Curriculum Focal Points* (2006), stresses multiplication and division of fractions and decimals, using ratios and applying proportionality, and developing the foundation for algebraic reasoning and thinking. The three problem types in this chapter provide multiple opportunities for middle school students to become highly engaged in mathematics learning and excited about the lessons.

BRAINTEASER PROBLEM EXAMPLE

Problem

Unit fractions are fractions with numerator of 1, such as 1/2, 1/3, and 1/4. When working with fractions, students frequently need to find equivalent fractions such as $1/2 = 2/4 = 4/8$, or $1/3 = 2/6 = 3/9$. For this brainteaser, the question is,

> Can unit fractions be renamed as a sum of unit fractions? And if so, how many can be found?

Mathematics Within the Problem

A natural question follows those stated in the preceding: Are there unit fractions for which it is impossible to rename them as a sum of unit fractions? As students begin their explorations, hopefully they will see that any multiple of the denominator of a given unit fraction always provides a way to write it as a sum of unit fractions. For example, consider the unit fraction $1/7$ where we provide an upper boundary of $28 = 7 \times 4$ for the denominators. Then, $1/7 = 1/14 + 1/14 = 1/14 + 1/28 + 1/28 = 1/28 + 1/28 + 1/28 + 1/28 = 1/21 + 1/21 + 1/21$.

There are four solutions, excluding rearrangement of fractions.

As another example, the unit fraction $1/2$ is equivalent to $2/4$. This fraction can be rewritten as the sum of unit fractions $1/4 + 1/4$. However, $1/4$ is equivalent to $2/8$, or $1/8 + 1/8$. As a result, $1/2$ can also be written as $1/8 + 1/8 + 1/8 + 1/8$. There are, then, an infinite number of responses, so a cap needs to be placed on the size of the denominator a fraction can be renamed. An acceptable denominator is 12, so $1/2 = 6/12$ would be the upper boundary for the denominator in this selected case.

Yet even with this limit, $1/2$ is not finished. First, $1/8 + 1/8 = 2/8 = 1/4$, so $1/4 + 1/8 + 1/8$ is also an acceptable answer. This process continues with other fractions equivalent to $1/2$ such as $3/6, 5/10$, and $6/12$. Again, selecting $1/2 = 3/6$ gives $1/2 = 1/6 + 1/6 + 1/6$ as well as $1/3 + 1/6$ (adding $1/6 + 1/6 = 2/6 = 1/3$).

Students need to be encouraged to explore many possibilities. For instance, when $1/2 = 6/12$ is selected, they should notice that 12 is a multiple of 3, 4, and 6. This opens up more opportunities. Students will likely begin with $1/2 = 1/12 + 1/12 + 1/12 + 1/12 + 1/12 + 1/12$. From this, the students can combine $1/12 + 1/12 = 2/12 = 1/6$, so another unit chain is $1/6 + 1/12 + 1/12 + 1/12 + 1/12$, and so is $1/6 + 1/6 + 1/12 + 1/12$.

From this point, students can combine $1/12 + 1/12 + 1/12 = 3/12 = 1/4$, and now the chain is $1/6 + 1/4 + 1/12$. Students can also combine $1/12 + 1/12 + 1/12 + 1/12 = 4/12 = 1/3$ and then rename $1/2$ as $1/3 + 1/12 + 1/12$.

Students may explore the following equivalent fractions:

$1/2 = 2/4 = 3/6 = 4/8 = 5/10 = 6/12$

$1/3 = 2/6 = 3/9 = 4/12$

$1/4 = 2/8 = 3/12$

$1/5 = 2/10$

$1/6 = 2/12$

Teachers may elect to reduce or raise the upper boundary on the denominator students are allowed to use based on the ability of the students.

Setting the Stage

A teacher defines and explains unit fractions and selects a few examples from the mathematics section in the preceding paragraphs to demonstrate to students. The teacher wants to be sure, without belaboring the point, that students recognize that more answers are expected than $1/2 = 1/4 + 1/4$, or $1/8 + 1/8 + 1/8 + 1/8$. Students are to locate as many chains as possible for each fraction within the upper boundary number specified.

Students are assigned to work in pairs or groups of three. They are encouraged to organize their work so they can later explain their thinking and demonstrate some of their unit fraction chains. The teacher announces the fractions students should use and the amount of time they have to explore.

Exploring

Students are provided time to work on finding as many unit fraction chains as they can within a set time. The teacher encourages students to explore each fraction deeply, looking for variety and uniqueness.

Summarizing

The teacher has students explain their methods for approaching the problem. Was there a particular method students used to help them find as many chains as possible? What is the longest chain (number of terms) a group found? What is the most unique chain any group thinks they found? Do students think their group discovered a chain no other group found?

The teacher may ask each student pair to combine with another pair to discuss the various unit chains they discovered. Through comparison and discussion, students will be checking their thinking and their mathematics.

Formative Assessment of Visible Thinking

The teacher moves about the room listening to students and watching them record their answers. The teacher wants to ensure that students are finding equivalent fractions. Students often begin adding denominators when performing addition with fractions. Students, when asked, should be able to successfully reevaluate the unit fractions to verify that they do indeed add up to the original unit fraction. For instance, students can demonstrate that $1/2 = 1/4 + 1/8 + 1/8$ by explaining that $1/8 + 1/8 = 2/8$ or $1/4$, and $1/4 + 1/4 = 2/4$ or $1/2$.

Connections to Strategies, Actions, and Conditions

Problems of this type support classroom strategies and actions that lead to effective classroom conditions. For strategies, teachers may use questioning, wait time, working in groups or pair-share, and interesting problems. For this particular problem, the actions would include such elements as enthusiasm, challenging work, active engagement, and transfer of learning. These strategies and actions support classroom conditions such as open discussion, metacognition, sense making, time to learn, and community of learners.

GROUP-WORTHY PROBLEM EXAMPLE

Problem

Mary and Paul want to meet for milkshakes at the mall. Mary walks 1 mile in 9 minutes, and Paul walks 1.5 miles in 11 minutes. Mary lives 1.2 miles from the mall, and Paul lives 1.4 miles from the mall.

If Mary and Paul want to arrive at the mall at the same time, what time (to the nearest second) should each one leave home for the mall?

Solve this problem in two different ways.

Mathematics Within the Problem

First Solution Possibility

One way the problem can be solved is by setting up proportions. Mary lives 1.2 miles from the mall and walks 1 mile in 9 minutes. For Mary, the proportion follows:

1 mile in 9 minutes is equal to 1.2 miles in x minutes.

$1/9 = 1.2/x$

$x = (9)(1.2)$

$x = 10.8$ minutes

Students need to convert 0.8 minutes into seconds. Again, they can set up a proportion:

8 is to 10 as x is to 60 seconds.

$8/10 = x/60$

$10x = 480$

$x = 48$ seconds

Mary needs 10 minutes 48 seconds to reach the mall.

Paul lives 1.4 miles from the mall and walks 1.5 miles in 11 minutes. Students set up a proportion and determine the following:

$1.4/x = 1.5/11$

$1.5x = 15.4$

$x = 10.27$ minutes (rounded)

Students need to convert 0.27 minutes to seconds. They can set up a proportion:

$27/100 = x/60$

$100x = 1{,}620$

$x = 16.2$ seconds

Paul needs about 10 minutes 16 seconds to reach the mall.

Students are not finished, since the problem asks when the two should leave their homes. Students may select any reasonable time for the two to leave their homes. Students may decide that Paul and Mary want to be at the mall at 4:30 p.m. and, thus, figure that Mary leaves home at 4:19:12 p.m., and Paul leaves at 4:19:44 p.m.

Still, students are not finished with the problem. Once they learn proportions (and cross products), students often have difficulty seeing the problem in a different way and then, in turn, solving it in a different way. Students might do this by setting up a table.

Second Solution Possibility

Since Mary lives 1.2 miles from the mall, students may decide to determine how long it takes Mary to travel 0.1 miles. With this unit measure, they can determine the time for 0.2 miles. Students know that 1 minute is 60 seconds, so 9 minutes is 540 seconds.

1 mile	9 minutes
1 mile	540 seconds. By dividing by 10, students note that Mary travels
0.1 mile	54 seconds, so she travels
0.2 mile	108 seconds (1 minute 48 seconds).

Mary travels the mile in 9 minutes, and the 0.2 mile in 1 minute 48 seconds. By combining these amounts, students determine that she needs 10 minutes 48 seconds to get to the mall.

Paul lives 1.4 miles from the mall and walks 1.5 miles in 11 minutes. Using the same idea, students want to find out how fast Paul walks 0.1 mile. Students may divide 1.5 by 15, and 660 seconds (11 times 60) by 15 to get 0.1 mile = 44 seconds.

1.5 miles	11 minutes or 660 seconds
0.1 mile	44 seconds (divide 1.5 and 660 by 15)
0.4 mile	176 seconds (multiply 44 by 4)
1 mile	440 seconds (multiply both 0.1 and 44 by 10)

Paul travels 1.4 miles in 440 seconds + 176 seconds (1 + 0.4 miles), or 616 seconds. Dividing by 60 gives an answer of 10.27 minutes, or 10 minutes 16 seconds (rounded).

Setting the Stage

A teacher forms students into groups of two or three and assigns the problem. The teacher emphasizes that students may round to the nearest second when determining when Mary and Paul should leave their houses. The teacher reminds students that two ways to solve the problem are needed. One calculator is assigned to each student pair or team. The teacher provides an estimated time for students to complete the problem.

Exploring

The teacher moves about the room helping students stay on track with cues or hints but not providing any answers. The teacher watches for unique or unusual solutions as well as traditional ones.

Summarizing

The teacher has students explain their thinking and their work. Several different student groups are selected to put their solutions on the board or overhead. Students not selected to place their problem solution on the board are encouraged to ask questions of the different groups.

Formative Assessment of Visible Thinking

The teacher should ask questions to various members of the groups to ensure that every student understands the mathematics. Questions such as the following can be targeted to students:

- How did you select the time for Paul and Mary to meet?
- What is a unit rate, and how is it helpful?
- How did you know that you needed to find 0.1 mile?

Connections to Strategies, Actions, and Conditions

Teachers may use strategies such as questioning, wait time, rubric scoring, working in groups, and engaging problems with a group-worthy problem of this nature. Actions such as continuous assessment, feedback, connections, challenging work, active engagement, and transfer of learning promote student thinking. These actions and strategies help support classroom conditions such as safe environment, open discussion, sense making, effort over innate ability, and high expectations.

TRANSFORMING PROBLEM EXAMPLE

Problem

Middle school students are frequently assigned to work problems that compare and order rational numbers, such as the following:

On the number line below, which number best represents P?

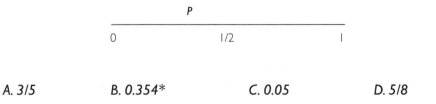

A. 3/5   B. 0.354*   C. 0.05   D. 5/8

Mathematics Within the Problem

Traditional Problem

The preceding problem is designed to tests students' understandings of rational numbers by having students identify and locate decimals and fractions on a number line. The problem works well as part of a summative test. Students should recognize that both A (3/5) and D (5/8) are greater than 1/2, so they cannot represent point *P* and are, therefore, not the answer. Students should also recognize that C (0.05) is very near 0, so it cannot be the answer. This leaves B (0.354). Students can quickly check their thinking by recalling that 1/2 is equal to 0.5, and halfway between 0 and 0.5 is 0.25. Since point *P* appears to be slightly more than halfway between 0 and 0.5, then 0.354 is a reasonable answer for *P*.

Students need to develop fluency in working with rational numbers by building a sense or feeling about the size of the number written as a fraction or decimal. One strong mathematical idea is for students to develop benchmarks of 0, 1, and 1/2 or 0.5. Students looking at a fraction or decimal should be able to readily recognize whether the fraction or decimal is greater than or less than 1/2 or 0.5.

Teachers may wish to provide practice opportunities to students by using flash-card representations of decimals and fractions. Teachers would select a card, show it to students, and then have all students signal "thumbs-up" for greater than 1, or "thumbs-down" for less than 1.

Transformed Problem

The teacher selects at random various fraction and decimal representations of numbers between 0 and 1. The fractions should relate to those students have been using such as thirds, fourths, fifths, sixths, and eighths. Decimals may be tenths, hundredths, or thousandths. The teacher identifies 10 to 15 examples of both fractions and decimals but an equal number of each. For instance, the teacher may select as fractions 1/3, 2/3, 1/5, 2/5, 3/5, 4/5, 1/6, 5/6, 1/8, 3/8, 5/8, and 7/8. For decimals, the teacher may select 0.1, 0.15, 0.275, 0.3, 0.4, 0.48, 0.55, 0.695, 0.745, 0.853, 0.955, and 0.99. The teacher may decide to use some equivalent representations such as 1/5 and 0.2 or 4/5 and 0.8.

Teachers should have available enough blank index cards and markers for each student to have 12 cards and a marker.

Setting the Stage

Students are formed into pairs. Each student pair is given a number line with 0, 1/2, and 1 marked on the line. Each student is provided with a marker and index cards. The teacher writes the fractions and decimals on the whiteboard or overhead. One student in the pair writes down the fractions on the blank index cards, and the other student writes down the decimals. Student pairs now have, in this example, 24 index cards with fractions and decimals. Students are also provided a calculator and, perhaps, fractions strips.

Exploring

The two sets of cards are combined and shuffled. Each student in the pair receives 12 cards dealt facedown. Students are to play three rounds of comparing. In the first round, students are trying to turn up a card with a number that is closer to 0 than their opponent's card. The student closer to 0 scores 1 point. Play continues for all 12 cards.

In the second round, the cards are reshuffled and redealt. Students are looking for numbers closer to 1. The student with the number closest to 1 scores 1 point. In the third round, cards are again reshuffled and redealt. Students are looking for the number closest to 1/2 or 0.5. Again, the student with the closest number scores 1 point.

During the exploring time, students play the three rounds. Calculators are used to settle any debates about who is closest. The teacher moves about the room listening to students as they play the game and discuss their thinking.

Summarizing

After students have played three rounds, the teacher helps them summarize their learning. The teacher asks the students:

- Which round (closest to 0, closest to 1, or closest to 1/2) do you think was the easiest? Why do you think this was the case?
- Which round did you find the most difficult? Why do you think this is the case?
- If I pull these two cards from the deck, what would you do to determine who won the point? (The teacher repeats this activity several times.)
- If I pull this card from the deck, how can I convert it to a fraction (if the card is a decimal) or a decimal (if the card is a fraction)? How does this information help me?

Formative Assessment of Visible Thinking

While moving about the room, the teacher has multiple opportunities to observe students and listen to their thinking. Students should not have to calculate some obvious fraction or decimal representations. If the students are calculating every card, the teacher needs to intervene. For instance, if the cards are 1/3 and 7/8 or 0.3 and 7/8, and the round is closest to 1 or 0, students should recognize 7/8 as the larger fraction and respond accordingly (closer to 1, further from 0).

The teacher may ask the student pairs to stop for a moment and think, because they can speed up the game when the decision is fairly obvious. The teacher asks students to place 7/8 on the number line where they think it would approximately be located by first asking whether 7/8 is greater than or less than 1/2. Students then place the 1/3 or 0.3 card on the number line with the teacher again asking if 1/3 or 0.3 is greater or less than 1/2. The teacher asks students to look at the order of fractions or decimals and determine their answer.

The teacher may then pick from several options to obtain additional formative data. The teacher may give the students a set of three numbers from their deck of cards, ask the students to locate the cards, and then place them in order on one of the students' desktops from greatest to least. The teacher would quickly walk around the room and confirm the students' work.

The teacher may also select three or more numbers, place the numbers on the whiteboard or overhead, and ask students to independently order the numbers on a piece of paper. Again, the teacher could move about the room checking or have the students turn in the completed paper. As another closure, teachers could have students write down their answers as before and trade papers with another team to confirm the answers.

Connections to Strategies, Actions, and Conditions

Strategies teachers may use include manipulatives, working in groups, peer tutoring, and engaging problems. Actions such as technology, connections, and active engagement encourage students to delve more deeply into the mathematics. These strategies and actions promote classroom conditions such as implemented curriculum, sense making, and self-assessment.

SUMMARY

Students need a variety of interesting and challenging problems to work. Mathematics is problem solving. Learning to use one's mathematical knowledge in unique situations greatly improves the odds that the mathematics will be remembered. Students also need time to think, reason, and struggle. Learning should not be considered something that takes no effort.

Students need time to discuss their ideas and to affirm their ideas are correct or immediately make adjustments in their thinking. Misunderstandings, once learned, are difficult to undo. The misunderstandings tend to remain with students once they have made the connections and placed the incorrect learning into long-term memory. Making thinking visible in classrooms is the best way for teachers to ensure correct learning is achieved and stored.

Part IV

Continuing the Work

11

How Do Teachers, Leaders, and Administrators Coordinate Their Efforts to Improve Mathematics Teaching and Learning?

T he probability is fairly high that most readers of this book have a background in elementary, secondary, or college level mathematics. If the readers are part of public or private school systems, they are most likely mathematics teachers, specialists, supervisors, or coordinators. Those who may not have a mathematics background are most likely assistant superintendents, principals, assistant principals, or curriculum directors. The positions all have responsibility for mathematics teaching and learning, some more directly than others. In order to help distinguish between responsibilities, we use the terms *mathematics leaders* for individuals with mathematics backgrounds and *administrators* for individuals who do not have a mathematics background.

Regardless of one's position within a school district, teachers, leaders, and administrators do not work in isolation. Teachers seeking to change their classroom strategies and conditions need the support of both leaders and administrators. If mathematics teachers want to increase visible thinking in their classrooms, they need a plan of action. A critical piece to that plan is communicating with leaders and administrators. As with any change initiative, there is a learning curve. Early attempts at instituting a new strategy will not be as successful as later ones. Teachers quickly lose interest in attempting change if, during the early stages of implementing something new, administrators or leaders inadvertently provide negative feedback. If administrators and leaders have not been kept informed of the changes, then negative feedback is likely.

At the same time, teachers often find it difficult to have meaningful conversations with administrators and leaders concerning content-specific ideas. This chapter provides an organized approach for conducting meaningful conversations about important topics to ensure that the efforts of teachers, leaders, and administrators are highly coordinated. We discuss four significant areas of coordination:

1. Working with administrators

2. Embedding lessons into the curriculum

3. Providing professional development

4. Co-planning and co-teaching

Just like the responsibilities of the personnel, these areas overlap by design.

WORKING WITH ADMINISTRATORS

In most schools, there tends to be a gap in an understanding of effective mathematics classrooms between teachers and leaders and also between teachers and administrators. Frequently, administrators base their expectations about mathematics achievement on their personal experiences. Even though these experiences may not have been positive, the assumption is that mathematics teaching and learning are just this way—the way the administrator experienced mathematics.

Common Goals and Expectations

Of utmost importance to achieving effective change is that teachers, leaders, and administrators agree on common goals and expectations concerning student learning and progress in mathematics. If everyone is not in agreement, then there are constant miscommunications and misconceptions that interfere with success. The following help to promote common goals and expectations:

- *Positive collegial relationships.* Collegial working relationships that are honest and supportive greatly influence an entire school climate. Good collegial relationships build positive rapport, and positive rapport provides a foundation for achieving common goals and objectives.
- *Consistent message.* Effective communication in positive collegial working conditions promotes a consistent message to everyone engaged in mathematics teaching and learning. A consistent message focuses on elements that are important, such as the mathematics curriculum and identified state standards. When assessment data point to apparent issues in mathematics learning within a school or district, all stakeholders need to hear and observe the same information for implementing change. In order to promote and sustain a consistent message, teachers, leaders, and administrators must talk and listen to all stakeholders. There must be a concerted effort to give everyone a voice. Teachers, leaders, and administrators should meet with small and large groups of faculty members, parents, and students. Using surveys without names or identification should also be considered.
- *Not about blame, no excuses.* In positive working, collegial relationships with consistent messages, teachers, leaders, and administrators do not focus on blame or excuses. They focus on success. The tone of every conversation is always about improving. There is no desire or intent to place fault or blame, only a strong desire to demonstrate improvement in mathematics teaching and learning.

Monitoring

Communication is very important. Most people do not realize that communication consists of two critical parts. Expectations are expressed through both words and actions. If no actions follow words, then the words are hollow. The odds are almost a sure bet that if monitoring does not occur, change does not occur. Teachers, leaders, and administrators need to monitor in two definite ways—through classroom visits and through the use of data and feedback.

Classroom Visits

Classroom visits should include teachers, leaders, and administrators. As long as classroom doors remain closed, the status quo will remain. Administrators often believe that every classroom visit is for teacher evaluation. Leaders are often unsure exactly what to do, and teachers are rarely allowed to visit classrooms beyond their own. This results in a serious breakdown in understanding effective classrooms and in clear expectations about mathematics teaching. Often, program implementation is not monitored. If teachers are expected to use specific strategies or materials as part of a change initiative, then their actions need to be monitored. The outcomes of monitoring are actually easy questions to ask and answer: Are the strategies and materials being used—and used effectively?

Administrators may feel that leaders are responsible for assuring the use of mathematics strategies and materials. If they are the only ones responsible, what happens to the consistent message from all stakeholders? Administrators may also believe that they are not able to supervise mathematics classrooms, especially at the secondary level, because this is not their area of training. However, the strategies, conditions, and actions identified in Figure 7.1 are observable by anyone. As a way to help shift the focus away from teacher evaluation to program implementation, administrators, leaders, and teachers should watch students for the best indicators of successful implementation. If the program uses effective instructional strategies such as those we have described throughout the book, then students should be actively engaged, discussing mathematics, and involved in grouping practices. One does not need a degree in mathematics to evaluate student participation and enthusiasm.

Data and Feedback

Teachers, leaders, and administrators also need to monitor through data analysis. Data are of no value if the data do not support altering actions. Actions cannot be effectively altered if there is no feedback. This cycle of data, feedback, and action is frequently broken.

While data come in many sizes and shapes, there are two very important forms of data that teachers, leaders, and administrators need to understand and use. These two forms are formative and summative. According to the National Research Council (2000), formative assessments—those ongoing assessments that make students' thinking visible to both teachers and students—are essential. In effectively using the ideas about visible thinking that we put forth, formative assessments are critical. Teachers are constantly gathering information about student learning. They use this data to make informed decisions about what actions to take next. Within a school, formative data are difficult to assess without classroom visits.

We identify summative data as that used to evaluate the degree of student learning after a period of time has passed. Summative data may be gathered on time frames such as weekly, monthly, every six or nine weeks, each semester, or annually. The most common forms of summative data are classroom test grades, grading period exams, district benchmark assessments, and state assessments. Summative data are used to look for patterns in learning, group strengths and weaknesses, content performance knowledge, and perhaps, error patterns through item analysis.

Effective leaders, administrators, and teachers rely heavily on formative and summative assessments as ways to evaluate student learning and instructional effectiveness. They understand the strengths and weaknesses of each data type and strive to be balanced in using data to inform practice. Teachers, administrators, and leaders need to ensure data are not one-sided. Boaler (2008) warns, "In addition to a reliance on multiple-choice formats, the mathematics tests used in most states across America are extremely narrow. They do not assess thinking, reasoning, or problem solving" (p. 87). Thinking, reasoning, and problem solving are skills that serve students well on all types of assessments, including state tests.

EMBEDDING LESSONS INTO THE CURRICULUM

Mathematics leaders need to work with teachers to correctly embed lessons and activities into the established curriculum. Lessons with related problems like the ones provided in this book are not "add-ons." Teachers are already pressed for time to cover the prescribed content; they cannot be asked to include additional lesson activities. Teachers should not be expected to make these instructional decisions in isolation.

With the examples we provide as a guide, teachers and leaders should gradually work to create and embed additional visible thinking problems. These additional problems should first focus on content areas where data indicate a lack of student learning. Leaders and administrators work with teachers to identify these areas, and then they provide time for teachers to collaboratively meet. During the meetings, leaders and teachers replace current lessons with ones that include visible thinking. Through this process, lesson balance is obtained, students' needs are better met, data are used to inform instruction, and weaknesses in student learning are addressed.

PROVIDING PROFESSIONAL DEVELOPMENT

Professional development is certainly a major part of any change initiative. Teachers, leaders, and administrators have not suffered a lack of professional development training sessions. However, there appears to be a fairly deep chasm between professional development training and changes in mathematics instruction. In blunt terms, the training is not transferring back into classrooms.

Elements of effective professional development have been researched and identified. Loucks-Horsley, Love, Stiles, Mundry, and Hewson (2003) have found that professional development

- Is driven by a well-defined image of effective classroom learning and teaching.
- Provides opportunities for teachers to build their content and pedagogical content knowledge and examine practice.
- Is research based and engages teachers as adult learners in the learning approaches they will use with their students.
- Provides opportunities for teachers to collaborate with colleagues and other experts to improve their practice.
- Supports teachers to serve in leadership roles.
- Links with other parts of the educational system.
- Has a design based on student learning data and is continuously evaluated and improved. (p. 44)

In addition to the preceding elements listed, there are other aspects of effective professional development that support the transferability of training into actions in mathematics classrooms. To achieve this, professional development needs to

- *Stay focused over time.* Far too often, professional development leaps from one educational fad to the next. Teachers barely have time to consider, much less adopt, use, and test, information and actions learned in professional development before other training is offered that either replaces or extends the previous training. This constant change leaves teachers and leaders confused and frustrated. The logical response from teachers is to just ignore any change request from professional development because they know it will be replaced soon.
- *Be based on how people change.* Research on how people change indicates that once an initiative has been adopted, people learn how to use the strategy or strategies in the initiative by progressing through distinct levels. Hall and Hord (2001) state that "change is a process, not an event. In other words, change is not accomplished by having a one-time announcement by an executive leader, a two-day training workshop for teachers in August, and/or the delivery of the new curriculum/technology. Instead change is a process

through which people and organizations move as they gradually come to understand, and become skilled and competent in the use of new ways" (p. 4).

- *Assist in transporting teachers.* Professional development needs to help supply pressure and support in moving teachers along the change continuum. Effective implementation of strategies or programs is not reached until everyone is correctly and effectively using the strategies or program elements.

- *Focus on identified short- and long-term goals.* Strategic planning is used within almost every school, often as a result of state mandates. Professional development sessions should focus on achieving the short- and long-term goals determined by stakeholders in the planning. Teachers need to know exactly how the training, and anticipated actions, translate into improved student achievement and fit the identified goals and objectives. Teachers and leaders need to know the expected behavior changes and outcomes that are gained from using a requested strategy.

- *Focus on student achievement.* Professional development should always focus on student achievement, learning, and success. Teachers, leaders, and administrators are all professionals hired to effectively and efficiently operate schools. Schools are institutions of learning for students. If the designated professional development training cannot be directly related to student achievement, it should not be offered.

- *Be designed to fit the theme of visible thinking.* One of the best litmus tests for professional development is visible thinking. If teachers initiate the recommended strategies or program, how will thinking be made visible as a result of these strategies or programs? The presence of visible thinking clearly links to effective instructional strategies, actions, and conditions. By enhancing visible thinking, students are more actively engaged, are more reflective, make more neural connections, and are better problem solvers.

Within this theme of visible thinking, teachers, with the guidance of mathematics leaders, need professional development time to design additional problems or scenarios that focus on visible thinking activities. These lessons need to be correctly placed into the established curriculum. Teachers and leaders also need to concentrate on supporting strategies and actions that directly influence student engagement and involvement. Teachers who are successfully using visible thinking activities are excellent resources and should be utilized to the fullest.

CO-PLANNING AND CO-TEACHING

Mathematics teachers and leaders need to be engaged in co-planning and co-teaching. Administrators need to actively support these actions. By being involved in co-planning and co-teaching, mathematics leaders gain tremendous insight into teacher knowledge and can assess what teachers obtained from professional development. Leaders can learn how to help teachers increase their pedagogical or mathematical knowledge and hone their instructional skills.

Co-planning

Co-planning is integral to visible thinking, and mathematics leaders are vital links between planning and making thinking visible. Course content has natural time divisions. These divisions are by the year, the semester, the grading period, and the week. Teachers need to intentionally assist students in understanding the content contained in the course, the sequence of the content, and the rationale for the sequence. Leaders need to be very involved in designing the sequence of the content.

At the beginning of the year, and at least every grading period thereafter, teachers need to help students make connections between the content already taught and the content to be taught. Teachers should spend time working with students to overview the course syllabus or table of contents. The highlighted content may be a review of previously taught and learned material, it may be an extension of previously taught and learned material, or it may be new to the students.

The overview provides time for students to look over chapter tests, chapter titles, and perhaps sample benchmark items. Discussion is about what vocabulary and content appears familiar and what does not. Discussion is also about expectations for performance. Students will be able to solve, demonstrate, show, calculate, prove, compare, or explain. A graphic of some nature that is displayed in the classroom and regularly referenced is extremely beneficial to visible thinking.

Co-teaching

Co-teaching offers leaders hands-on experience. Co-teaching is not demonstration teaching where the leaders "show" the teachers "how it's done." In co-teaching, leaders work with teachers to teach the planned lesson. Neither the teacher nor the leader has time to sit down and watch.

Co-teaching is ideal for helping teachers launch a new strategy. Through this joint effort, teachers have another pair of hands to assist in their classrooms. In co-teaching, both teachers and leaders are learners. There are two sets of eyes to watch students' reactions and two sets of ears to listen to students' conversations. Co-teaching builds rapport and empathy. Reflection upon the success of a lesson is easier when the lesson was co-taught.

Administrators may not be comfortable or have the content knowledge to co-teach mathematics lessons. This is perfectly reasonable. Administrators cannot be experts in every content area. Nonetheless, effective administrators can actively support and encourage both co-planning and co-teaching through their words and actions. Because they know co-planning and co-teaching are beneficial to everyone, not just to new hires or first-year teachers, administrators work to help teachers and leaders find time to engage in these actions.

SUMMARY

Teachers need support from both leaders and administrators if they are to effectively use visible thinking strategies and activities with their students. They have a difficult enough job without receiving mixed messages from leaders and administrators. Consistent messages come from visiting classrooms, collegial conversations, sharing data, and providing worthwhile professional development. Teachers need to regularly hear positive feedback resulting from their efforts.

Teachers, leaders, and administrators need to operate in a "no blame, no excuse" zone. Actions related to blaming or excusing increase dissonance and displace responsibility. Blaming and excusing infer that nothing can be done to improve. Nothing is further from the truth.

The ideas about visible thinking discussed throughout this book relate to communication. How do students communicate their understanding of mathematics? By incorporating visible thinking strategies into daily lessons, teachers will observe changes in student learning. Those changes will make a difference in closing the achievement gap in mathematics.

Appendix A

Research Support for Visible Thinking Strategies, Conditions, and Actions

Strategies	Resources
Interesting, engaging problems	National Research Council, 2004
Questioning	Marzano, Pickering, and Pollock, 2001
Wait time	Marzano, Pickering, and Pollock, 2001
Manipulatives	Wagner, 2005; Van de Walle, 2004
Vocabulary development	Wagner, 2005
Graphic organizers	Marzano, Pickering, and Pollock, 2001
Pair-share	Van de Walle, 2004
Working in groups	Jensen, 1998; Van de Walle, 2004
Peer tutoring	Wagner, 2005
Journal writing	Van de Walle, 2004
Rubric scoring	Hunter, 2004

Conditions	Resources
Safe environment	Marzano, 2003
Open discussions	National Council of Teachers of Mathematics, 2000
Aligned curriculum	English, 2000; Marzano 2003
Implemented curriculum	English, 2000
Metacognition	National Research Council, 1999, 2000
Sense making	National Research Council, 1999, 2002, 2004, 2005
Self-assessment	National Research Council, 1999, 2002, 2004, 2005
Time to learn	Marzano, 2003; National Council of Teachers of Mathematics, 2000
Community of learners	Boaler, 2006
Effort over innate ability	Dweck, 2006; National Research Council, 2002
High expectations	Reeves, 2006; Stronge, 2007

Actions	Resources
Opportunity to learn	Marzano, 2003
Active engagement	National Research Council, 2001, 2002, 2004, 2005
Enthusiasm	Stronge, 2007
Challenging work	National Research Council, 2001, 2002, 2004, 2005
Class participation	National Research Council, 2001, 2002, 2004, 2005
Technology inclusion	National Council of Teachers of Mathematics, 2000
Connections	National Council of Teachers of Mathematics, 2000; National Research Council, 1999, 2000, 2002, 2005
Transfer of learning	National Research Council, 1999, 2000
Continuous assessment	National Mathematics Advisory Panel, 2008; Conzemius and O'Neill, 2001
Feedback	Marzano, 2003; National Research Council, 1999, 2000
Variety of strategies	Boaler, 2006; Marzano, 2003; National Research Council, 2002

Appendix B

Lessons Using Technology:
Additional Materials

VISIBLE THINKING WITH A GRAPHING CALCULATOR FOR ELEMENTARY AND MIDDLE GRADES

Lesson Activity

"Marie rides her bicycle every weekend at the park. She has trained herself to set a pace of about 4 mph. If she maintains this rate of speed over time, what are some possible distances that she could ride each day?" How far could she ride in 7 hours? How far could she ride in 8 1/2 hours?

Using representations to facilitate visual thinking—including verbal (descriptive), numeric, graphical (geometric), and symbolic (algebraic) forms of the same data—let's take a look at some of the models of data that are available for visual thinking when using a graphing calculator to solve this problem. Noted here are nine different forms of the same data set spanning grade levels from Grade 3 to Grade 8 (and pre-algebra). Remember, however, it is not the calculator itself that is essential to the lesson. The calculator is a tool to easily and quickly display visual data to help facilitate various discussions between students (and groups of students) about the mathematics and ways to organize and understand the data. The way students think about the data is the key to student understanding, learning, and achievement.

| ```
4                    4
4+4                  8
4+4+4               12
4+4+4+4             16
4+4+4+4+4           20
4+4+4+4+4+4         24
█
``` | 1. In this example we see a display showing the use of repeated addition. Typically this is an introduction, for upper elementary students, to multiplication. It matches well to the use of manipulatives as you can see one group of four represented. The four could be single blocks, a set of four blocks, four miles as distance, four miles per hour as a rate, etc. The second line shows two sets of four or four miles traveled twice—then three groups, four groups, five groups, etc. Students can also begin to look at arithmetic sequences and discuss terms in a sequence or set. |
| ```
1*4                  4
2*4                  8
3*4                 12
4*4                 16
5*4                 20
6*4                 24
``` | 2. This screen shows the use of multiplication as an extension to the previous example. The multiplier is the number of groups or number of times a group of four occurs; the multiplicand is a constant representing 4 miles traveled in an hour, and the product is the total amount of objects in each group (blocks, sets, miles, and so on). This example also serves as an introduction to terms in a sequence—the first term or first element in the data set is 4, the second term/element is 8, the third term/element is 12, etc. |
| ```
L1      L2      🔳    3
 0       0      ------
 1       4
 2       8
 3      12
 4      16
 5      20
 6      24

L3 =
``` | 3. This illustration (a numeric representation of the data) shows the use of the List Editor feature of the TI-73 Explorer graphing calculator and is very similar to other graphing calculators available in school districts. The data noted is another representation of the problem solving situation noted above. In some cases teachers refer to this as a "T" chart commonly used in algebra to evaluate an expression or an equation. List #1 (L1) represents the number of hours that Marie could ride her bicycle, and List #2 (L2) represents the number of miles traveled at a rate of 4 miles per hour. |
| ```
HOURS   MILES   ▬▬▬   3
 0       0
 1       4
 2       8
 3      12
 4      16
 5      20
 6      24

Name=█
``` | 4. This screen is similar to the previous screen but allows students and teachers to name the lists as the real-world objects that are represented. This screen also provides the opportunity to introduce the concept of independent and dependent variables. The number of hours could be represented by the variable $x$, and the number of miles represented by the variable $y$, using symbolic notation. The number of miles traveled ($y$) would be dependent on the number of hours traveled ($x$) at an average speed of 4 mph. |

Plot1 Plot2 Plot3 \Y₁■4X \Y₂■4X+0 \Y₃= \Y₄=	5. Using the "Y=" menu on the calculator, the expression could now be represented as a symbolic algorithm (algebraic representation) using the variables noted in Example 4. The number of miles traveled (Y) equals 4 (the rate of miles traveled per hour) times the number of hours (X). This is known as the "slope intercept form" of an algebraic equation. 4X and 4X + 0 are equivalent, with "0" representing the starting point of zero miles traveled at the beginning of Maria's weekend bicycle riding event.

X	Y₁	Y₂
5	20	20
6	24	24
7	28	28
8	32	32
9	36	36
10	40	40
11	44	44

X=11

6. Once an equation has been entered into the "Y=" menu of the graphing calculator, a table of data representing the range of Maria's bicycle travel can be created. This table can be modified by using various calculator menus to represent fractional or decimal amounts that yield more realistic distances traveled. Marie does not always travel exactly 4 miles each hour.

X	Y₁	Y₂
6.5	26	26
6.75	27	27
7	28	28
7.25	29	29
7.5	30	30
7.75	31	31
8	32	32

X=8

7. Here is an example of the same table, but the change between times traveled is now set for 1/4 or 0.25 of an hour rather than whole numbers. Amounts such as 6 1/2 hours of travel or decimal fractions such as 7.75 hours of travel can be displayed. Students can change the parameters on the calculator to match the values used in the real-world situation. Note that the values for "Y₁" and "Y₂" are equivalent as 4X and 4X + 0 are equivalent.

P1:L1,L2

X=1   Y=4

8. Using the Statistical Plot (Plot) menu, students can select a variety of graphical representations to organize the data. Noted here is a scatterplot showing the (discrete) data used in the original problem—one hour traveled at four miles per hour, two hours traveled at four miles per hour, etc. The trace feature of the graphing calculator has been turned on to display the first point in the data set using the variables "X" for hours and "Y" for total miles traveled.

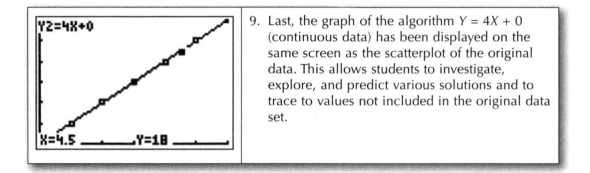

9. Last, the graph of the algorithm $Y = 4X + 0$ (continuous data) has been displayed on the same screen as the scatterplot of the original data. This allows students to investigate, explore, and predict various solutions and to trace to values not included in the original data set.

Using multiple representations of data with technology, such as graphing calculators, students can use visible thinking to discuss different forms of data and to explore a variety of problem solving strategies.

Source: Lesson created by Texas Instruments and Robb Wilson (2010), TI Educational Technology Consultant.

CASIO CALCULATOR LESSON (FIGURE 4.4): HANDOUT

Part A: Review order of operations.

1. **PEMDAS** is a way to remember the rules for order of operations.

2. First complete within **P**_____

3. Then do **E**_____

4. Next **M**_____

5. Finally **A**_____

Evaluate the following equations:

$60 \div (12 + 3) =$ ___

$53 + 15 \times (6^2 \div 9) =$ ___

$(8 \times 2^3 - 5)^3 =$ ___

$(6^2 - 15 \div 3) \times 2^2 =$ ___

$42 + 3 \times (5^2 - 21) =$ ___

Part B: Explore and discuss.

1. Place the missing parentheses:

$17 + 4 \times 54 - 42 = 65$

$918 - 12^2 \times 22 - 4^2 = 17{,}012$

$712 - 4^3 + 8^2 \times 52 - 7^2 = 328$

$94 - 13 + 4^2 - 2 \times 9 = 207$

$8^2 + 36 \div \sqrt{9} + 2 = 78$

2. Write your own missing parentheses problem with its correct answer here. Write it without parentheses on a separate piece of paper and give it to a classmate to solve.

ANSWER PAGE FOR EXPLORING ORDER OF OPERATIONS WITH CALCULATORS

Part A: Review order of operations.

1. **PEMDAS** is a way to remember the rules for order of operations.

2. First complete within **Parentheses**

3. Then do **Exponents (powers or roots)**

4. Next **Multiply or Divide left to right**

5. Finally **Add or Subtract left to right**

Evaluate the following equations:

$60 \div (12 + 3) = 4$

$53 + 15 \times (6^2 \div 9) = 113$

$(8 \times 2^3 - 5)^3 = 205{,}379$

$(6^2 - 15 \div 3) \times 2^2 = 124$

$42 + 3 \times (5^2 - 21) = 54$

Part B: Explore and discuss.

1. Place the missing parentheses:

$17 + 4 \times (54 - 42) = 65$

$(918 - 12^2) \times 22 - 4^2 = 17{,}012$

$712 - (4^3 + 8^2) \times (52 - 7^2) = 328$

$94 - 13 + (4^2 - 2) \times 9 = 207$

$8^2 + (36 \div \sqrt{9} + 2) = 78$

2. Write your own missing parentheses problem with its correct answer here. Write it without parentheses on a separate piece of paper and give it to a classmate to solve.

References

Boaler, J. (2002). *Experiencing school mathematics: Traditional and reform approaches to teaching and their impact on student learning.* Mahwah, NJ: Erlbaum.

Boaler, J. (2006, January). Urban success: A multidimensional mathematics approach with equitable outcomes. *Phi Delta Kappan, 87*(5), 364–369.

Boaler, J. (2008). *What's math got to do with it? Helping children learn to love their least favorite subject.* New York, NY: Penguin.

Brooks, J., & Brooks, M. (1999). *In search of understanding: The case for constructivist classrooms.* Alexandria, VA: Association for Supervision and Curriculum Development.

Casio America, Inc., & Pittock, J. (2010). *Exploring order of operations with calculators.* Unpublished manuscript.

Common Core State Standards. (2010). Retrieved June 22, 2010, from www.corestandards .org

Conzemius, A., & O'Neill, J. (2001). *Building shared responsibility for student learning.* Alexandria, VA: Association for Supervision and Curriculum Development.

Cushman, K. (2003). *Fires in the bathroom: Advice for teachers from high school students.* New York, NY: New Press.

DuFour, R., DuFour, R., Eaker, R., & Karhanek, G. (2004). *Whatever it takes: How professional learning communities respond when kids don't learn.* Bloomington, IN: National Educational Service.

Dweck, C. (2006). *Mindset: The new psychology of success.* New York, NY: Random House.

English, F. (2000). *Deciding what to teach and test.* Thousand Oaks, CA: Corwin.

ExploreLearning. (2010). Square roots. In *Grade 6–8 Exploration Guide.* Available from www.explorelearning.com

Grouws, D., & Cebulla, K. (2000). *Improving student achievement in mathematics.* Geneva, Switzerland: International Academy of Education.

Gutierrez, R. (2000). Advancing African American urban youth in mathematics: Unpacking the success of one math department. *American Journal of Education, 109,* 63–111.

Hall, G., & Hord, S. (2001). *Implementing change: Patterns, principles, and potholes.* Needham Heights, MA: Allyn & Bacon.

Hunter, R. (2004). *Madeline Hunter's mastery teaching: Increasing instructional effectiveness in elementary and secondary schools.* Thousand Oaks, CA: Corwin.

Jensen, E. (1998). *Teaching with the brain in mind.* Alexandria, VA: Association for Supervision and Curriculum Development.

Jensen, E. (2008, February). A fresh look at brain-based learning. *Phi Delta Kappan, 89*(6), 408–417.

Kennedy, M. (2005). *Inside teaching: How classroom life undermines reform.* Cambridge, MA: Harvard University Press.

Loucks-Horsley, S., Love, N., Stiles, K., Mundry, S., & Hewson, P. (2003). *Designing professional development for teachers of science and mathematics.* Thousand Oaks, CA: Corwin.

Marshall, J. (2006, January). Math wars 2: It's the teaching, stupid! *Phi Delta Kappan, 87*(5), 356–363.

Marzano, R. (2003). *What works in schools: Translating research into action.* Alexandria, VA: Association for Supervision and Curriculum Development.

Marzano, R., Pickering, D., & Pollock, J. (2001). *Classroom instruction that works: Research-based strategies for increasing student achievement.* Alexandria, VA: Association for Supervision and Curriculum Development.

National Center for Education Statistics. (2009). *NAEP Data Explorer.* Available from http://nces.ed.gov

National Commission on Mathematics and Science Teaching for the 21st Century. (2000). *Before it's too late: A report to the nation from the National Commission on Mathematics and Science Teaching for the 21st Century.* Washington, DC: U.S. Department of Education.

National Council of Teachers of Mathematics. (2000). *Principles and standards for school mathematics.* Reston, VA: Author.

National Council of Teachers of Mathematics. (2006). *Curriculum focal points.* Reston, VA: Author.

National Council of Teachers of Mathematics. (2009). *Focus on high school mathematics: Reasoning and sense making.* Reston, VA: Author.

National Mathematics Advisory Panel. (2008). *Foundations for success: The final report of the National Mathematics Advisory Panel.* Washington, DC: U.S. Department of Education.

National Research Council. (1999). *Improving student learning: A strategic plan for education research and its utilization.* Washington, DC: National Academy Press.

National Research Council. (2000). *How people learn: Brain, mind, experience, and school.* Washington, DC: National Academy Press.

National Research Council. (2001). *Adding it up: Helping children learn mathematics.* Washington, DC: National Academy Press.

National Research Council. (2002). *Helping children learn mathematics.* Washington, DC: National Academy Press.

National Research Council. (2004). *Engaging schools: Fostering high school students' motivation to learn.* Washington, DC: National Academy Press.

National Research Council. (2005). *How students learn: History, mathematics, and science in the classroom.* Washington, DC: National Academy Press.

Organisation for Economic Co-operation and Development. (2007). *Programme for International Student Assessment: PISA 2006: Science competencies for tomorrow's world.* Retrieved from www.pisa.oecd.org/dataoecd/30/17/39703267.pdf

Perkins, D. (2003). *Making thinking visible. New horizons for learning.* Retreived from www.newhorizons.org/strategies/thinking/perkins.htm

Reeves, D. (2006). *The leaning leader: How to focus school improvement for better results.* Alexandria, VA: Association for Supervision and Curriculum Development.

Ritchhart, R., & Perkins, D. (2008, February). Making thinking visible. *Educational Leadership, 65*(5), 57–61.

Sousa, D. (2008). *How the brain learns mathematics.* Thousand Oaks, CA: Corwin.

Stronge, J. (2007). *Qualities of effective teachers.* Alexandria, VA: Association for Supervision and Curriculum Development.

Texas Instruments & Wilson, R. (2010). *Using a graphing calculator to model real-world situations.* Unpublished manuscript.

Urbina, I. (2010, January 11). As school exit tests prove tough, states ease standards. *New York Times.* Available from www.nytimes.com

Van de Walle, J. (2004). *Elementary and middle school mathematics: Teaching developmentally.* Boston, MA: Pearson.

Wagner, S. (Ed.). (2005). *PRIME: PRompt intervention in mathematics education.* Columbus: Ohio Resource Center for Mathematics, Science, and Reading & Ohio Department of Education.

Willis, J. (2008, February). Building a bridge from neuroscience to the classroom. *Phi Delta Kappan, 89*(6), 424–427.

Wolfe, M. (2005). Using assessments to support learning. In S. Wagner (Ed.), *PRIME: PRompt intervention in mathematics education* (pp. 177–198). Columbus: Ohio Resource Center for Mathematics, Science, and Reading & Ohio Department of Education.

Index

CORWIN
A SAGE Company

The Corwin logo—a raven striding across an open book—represents the union of courage and learning. Corwin is committed to improving education for all learners by publishing books and other professional development resources for those serving the field of PreK–12 education. By providing practical, hands-on materials, Corwin continues to carry out the promise of its motto: **"Helping Educators Do Their Work Better."**

The National Council of Teachers of Mathematics is a public voice of mathematics education, supporting teachers to ensure equitable mathematics learning of the highest quality for all students through vision, leadership, professional development, and research.